THE BEST IN

SPECIALIST

PACKAGING DESIGN

THE BEST IN

SPECIALIST

PACKAGING DESIGN

STAFFORD CLIFF

ROTOVISION

A QUARTO BOOK

Published by ROTOVISION SA
Route Suisse 9
CH-1295 Mies
Switzerland

ISBN 2-88046-162-6

This book was designed and produced by
Quarto Publishing plc
6 Blundell Street
London N7 9BH

Creative Director: Richard Dewing
Designer: Chris Dymond
Editor: Susan Berry
Picture Researcher: Michele Faram

Typeset in Great Britain by
Central Southern Typesetters, Eastbourne
Manufactured in Singapore by Eray Scan Pte. Limited
Printed in Hong Kong by Leefung-Asco Printers Ltd

Stafford Cliff would like to acknowledge the help of the following
people in the compilation of this book: Kulbir Thandi, Jonathan Scott,
Priscilla Carluccio, Beth Nelson, Virginia Pepper,
Stephen Paul and Dany Arnoud.

Contents

Introduction

For the purpose of this book, I have defined specialist packaging as that which is created for a specific product or adapted from an existing form, with special lids, handles, boxes or sleeves. Materials, textures or finishes can make a traditional form appear unique. Orange juice packed in a bottle that uses a texture reminiscent of the fruit peel can make the customer respond unconsciously. Motor oil in grey metallic-looking containers that echo engine styling will communicate masculine connotations in the same way that sensual glass perfume bottles and pearlized finishes on shampoo and bath oil bottles give a rich feminine feel, particularly when used with pastel colours.

Fit for the purpose The work included in this book has been chosen as a broad cross-section of its kind – sometimes because of its excellent use of type and illustration, sometimes for the sheer pleasure of the form, and sometimes because of its inspirational nature. I'm sure you will think of other examples. There are some key elements every design should include: it should describe its contents and be suitable for the purpose; it should be distinctive and adaptable if it is part of a range; it should be legal; and it should stand out.

The design of a pack can give tremendous shelf appeal, as well as an added boost to sales. On the crowded shelves of supermarkets, every product is jostling for attention with its neighbours. Sometimes minor brands are designed to duplicate, as closely as legally possible, the look of the brand

leader. Sometimes manufacturers strive to make the shape and the graphics as different as possible from all the competition. The size of the "facing" (front surface); the number of "facings" on a shelf (and the effect that repetition of the product gives); the type of colours (and people's reaction to certain colours); and the effect store lighting has on colours are all elements to consider. We know from the reams of consumer research that a housewife will react to certain products seen for only a fraction of a second, and certain colours are considered sacrosanct for certain foods.

Own-brand packaging In the 1970s supermarkets led a rearguard action with own-brand packaging. Sainsbury's stores in the UK had already created a reputation for excellence in house pack designs, with the re-packaging of products of which many were by the brand leaders. These designs reflected the image of the store rather than the image of the manufacturer. Now, products that ranged across all aspects of food and non-comestibles were packed to look alike or coordinate.

Sometimes an "own brand" product was shown side by side with main brand products, and of course tests were done and sales figures carefully monitored. Supermarkets like the French Carréfour, the British International and the American Grand Union all developed "no brand concepts". The idea involved simple one or two colour typographic designs on white back-grounds, utilizing existing packaging forms, and rejecting the use of any decoration, illustration, or photography. In some cases, even the name of

the store was omitted. The success relied heavily on the reputation and the integrity of the store and its pricing policy. "No money has been wasted on packaging or over-glamorizing these products", they seemed to be saying, "and we are passing the cost-saving on to you". The irony was that in many cases the packs and labels had to be produced on machines set up to print four or five colours whether you wanted them or not.

Twenty years later, the Japanese chain MUJI are pursuing the same route, with their "no label" style of packaging, but now it seems to fit with the eco-smart generation of today.

Recycling packaging Packaging legislation is currently an issue of immense worldwide concern. Conferences are held and EC papers are issued on the effect of packaging (especially over-packaging) on the environment. Recent research in one EC country has shown that 94 per cent of consumers questioned thought that many items were over-packaged, and that the Government should introduce laws to force manufacturers to use recycled (or to recycle) materials. At the same time 51 per cent refused to pay more for recycled goods, only 36 per cent buy "green" products, and only 35 per cent take the trouble to recycle bottles or newspapers.

In Germany, the "Polluter pays" or "Duales system" has had a dramatic and widespread effect. Launched in 1990, legislation states that "packaging shall be manufactured from materials which are environmentally compatible", and that packaging "is restricted in volume and weight to the dimensions actually required to protect the contents and to market the product". The voluntary scheme is strictly monitored, and licensed companies include a specially designed "green dot" logo on their pack. Many products feature outer protective containers that can be removed by the customer and left in bins outside the stores.

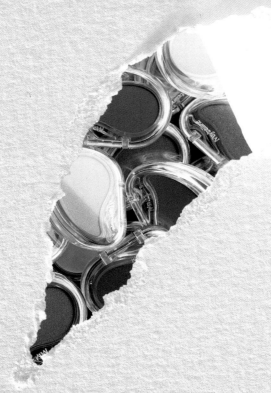

However this does not lead to any noticeable reduction in waste, compared to a system involving the collection (by private contractors) of recyclable materials from specially provided bins outside peoples' homes. Consumers divide their packaging waste into three categories: bottle bank, wastepaper bin, and packaging bin — where plastics, laminates and metal go.

Breaking the mould All this sounds like hard work, and requires a commitment on behalf of the public, and Germany is the only country so far to have adapted such a far-sighted scheme. They predict the results will be millions of tons less waste and they plan to extend the scheme to include mail order and PR material (and newspapers), and eventually electrical products and automobiles. It can only be a matter of time before the rest of the world follows their lead. Much depends on the relevant Government, and on EC legislation in Europe and the cooperation of industry. But the designer has an important role to play in this scenario too. Often designers are given a very tight brief. Sometimes slight modifications can be made to a pack to make it more individual, but new mouldings for plastic and glass containers can be extremely expensive and can usually only be justified for products with extremely high runs, such as detergents, shampoos or soft drinks. But at other times, the designer has the opportunity to totally rethink the form that the pack takes, and this is where environmental issues can also be considered.

Often the lead is taken by smaller retailers who have more flexibility, or are prepared to experiment. Ideas can also come from smaller manufacturers, producing small quantities – sometimes even hand-packed items. The last chapter in this book looks at this area of packaging – products that sell only because of their packaging – in other words, those in which the pack is sometimes more important and more desirable than the product it contains. Although nobody buys scent without first smelling the contents, or being loyal to a certain fragrance, customers are certainly enticed initially by the often extravagant and sensual design of the bottle. New brands are launched as much on the design of the container as they are on the scent of the contents, or the charisma of the "personality" behind it. But ultimately it's still a bottle in a box.

The chapter on eclectic packaging examines the emotions involved in responding to combinations of highly fashionable items, products such as soap or stationery, wrapped in a leaf, tied with rough twine and sealed in a bag with a couple of sea shells and a twig pencil or a seed-pod. The price of the note paper, or the quality of it, becomes unimportant compared to the image that the items create, and the way we respond to it.

Customer reaction After all, packaging is ultimately a question of response. We respond to chocolate when it's in a red pack and cigarettes when they are in a gold pack. We are used to seeing beer in tin cans and wine in glass bottles. We like to have matches in cardboard (or better still wooden) boxes and orange juice in plastic bottles. And when these traditions are changed, we notice it.

We also notice the extra care and attention a manufacturer has taken to make a product easier to carry or to pour, to ensure it is resealable, and to prevent it from tipping over. If the graphics are better designed and executed, the orange juice seems to be better quality; if the biscuits are in a tin rather than in a packet, they feel more "special". At the same time, if breakfast cereal came in this form, it would seem over-packaged and inappropriate, even if it were offered at the same price.

So "fitness for purpose" has an important role to play in all this. Some products seem so ideally suited that we can't imagine them better presented, and it would be foolish to try. Others cry out for someone to take a good look at their method of containment. Which of us has not been frustrated by those tiny packs of milk on airlines? And I'd like a pound for every student who's shown me a new way to pack a light bulb!

We become unconsciously involved with packs, and can become quite emotional if we see again a pack remembered from childhood. If a container we've always known suddenly gets redesigned, it can make us angry and even stop us from buying it.

Finally, packaging can give us great pleasure. Designers will go on trying to identify what makes a great classic — like the Cocacola and the champagne bottle, the sardine can with a key and the ubiquitous egg box. Perhaps it is because we see these designs from the perspective of time that our image of them is mixed with memories we associate with them, and the image that advertising has given them. Perhaps it is because it was the first time that a certain shape, like the Perrier bottle, was used, and forever after we associate its imitators with it. And perhaps it is that every now and then someone comes up with a pack that is so against all the trends, so contrary to our expectations at the time, and so functional in its performance and so memorable, quirky, lovable or strange that we'll all want it right away (providing the price is right, too).

Coordinated The combined effect of several products displayed together on a shelf, all sporting the same design, can multiply the impact enormously, even if the design is modified to differentiate between varying ingredients, or if pack sizes and materials vary. Colour, typography and illustration all help to carry recognition. Sometimes, the entire range will be displayed together, on one merchandizing unit. But at other times, products might be sold in different departments and bought by different customers. Advertising can help to build product range recognition, so that when the customer sees the product, its individuality will make it memorable.

Sometimes, the manufacturer will have a corporate look, to be applied like an identity across all its products. But at other times the range itself — be it haircare or tea, banking or biscuits — will be given its own identity, crafted to appeal to its target market and price range.

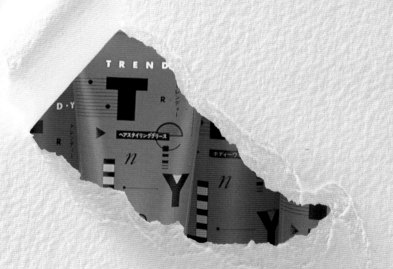

Arran Provisions
Gift Packs

CLIENT: Arran Provisions, Glasgow, Scotland, UK

DESCRIPTION OF PRODUCT: Labelling and packaging for range of preserves, mustards and marmalades, individually and gift packed

DESIGNER: Graphic Partners, Edinburgh, Scotland, UK

DATE OF COMPLETION: 1988

TARGET MARKET: Speciality gift market

PLACE OF SALE: Speciality gift shops and delicatessens

CLIENT'S BRIEF: To reposition the range upmarket and create themed groupings.

DESIGN RATIONALE: Designs emphasize added-value products. Naive decorative style underscores traditional, hand-crafted nature of products.

Asda Cooking Oils

CLIENT: Asda Stores Limited, Leeds, UK

DESCRIPTION OF PRODUCT: Range of own-label cooking oils, using PET in litre-size for ordinary oils and glass in 250 and 500ml sizes for speciality oils.

DESIGNER: Graham Lincoln & Partners, Northampton, UK

ILLUSTRATOR OR PHOTOGRAPHER: David Westwood

DATE OF COMPLETION/PRODUCT LAUNCH: 1986

TARGET MARKET: B, C1, C2, D (principally female consumers)

PLACE OF SALE: Asda Supermarkets

CLIENT'S BRIEF: To develop a visual identity for a complete range of cooking oils covering mass market and speciality varieties whose common denominator is natural purity.

DESIGN RATIONALE: To unify the range, accounting for differing sizes of pack format, to emphasize the natural element with flora and to emphasize the purity with the "homemade" device of the handwritten product description within the border.

Nature's Compliments

CLIENT: J Sainsbury's PLC, London, UK

DESCRIPTION OF PRODUCT: Men's toiletries range –
various shapes and sizes

DESIGNER: Aftershave bottle designed by Planet (Ian
Webb). Graphics designed by Worthington & Co
(Salvatore Cicero), London, UK

DATE OF COMPLETION/PRODUCT LAUNCH: November
1991

TARGET MARKET: ABC group: men aged 25 to 45 (and
women purchasing for them)

PLACE OF SALE: Sainsbury's multiple stores

CLIENT'S BRIEF: A quality product to appeal to
appropriate market. Premium price (slight) over other
own label and branded products stocked by store. Range
extension to successful women's range.

DESIGN RATIONALE: To meet the client's brief – simple,
clean quality statement to provide non 'own label' feel
and to sit competitively with branded products.

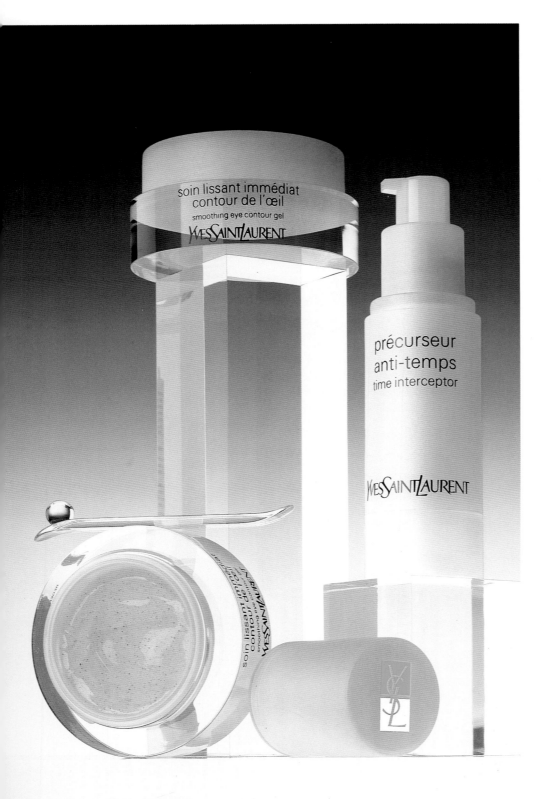

Soin, Précurseur de Beauté

CLIENT: Yves Saint Laurent Parfums, Neuilly sur Seine, France

DESCRIPTION OF PRODUCT: Full skincare line

DESIGNER: Jerome Faillant-Dumas – Art Director/Benoit Gillan/Yves Saint Laurent, Neuilly sur Seine, France

PHOTOGRAPHER: Andre Rau (Model)/Peter Knaup (Still Life)

DATE OF COMPLETION/PRODUCT LAUNCH: March 1992

TARGET MARKET: Worldwide

PLACE OF SALE: Department stores and chosen Yves Saint Laurent perfumeries

masque clarté
immédiate
instant clarifying masque

YvesSaintLaurent

précurseur
anti-temps
time interceptor

soin lissant immédiat
contour de l'œil
smoothing eye contour gel

YvesSaintLaurent

masque crème hydro actif
hydro-active moisture masque

YvesSaintLaurent

tonique
soin pureté
oil-control tonic

tonique
soin fraîcheur
mild clarifying tonic

tonique
soin douceur
extra-gentle tonic

nutri vitale nuit enrichie
intensive nighttime revitalizer

YvesSaintLaurent

YvesSaintLaurent

nutri vitale nuit
nighttime revitalizer

YvesSaintLaurent

gel mousse
pureté
foaming cleansing gel

crème
démaquillante
douceur
soothing creme cleanser

hydra vitale jour enrichie
hydro-intensive day creme

YvesSaintLaurent

lait
démaquillant
fraîcheur
instant cleansing milk

YvesSaintLaurent

YvesSaintLaurent

hydra vitale jour
hydro-light day creme

YvesSaintLaurent

YvesSaintLaurent

Trendy

CLIENT: Shiseido, Tokyo, Japan

DESCRIPTION OF PRODUCT: Trendy men's toiletries

DESIGNER: Pentagram/Kenneth Grange/Mervyn Kurlansky/Lars Baecklund/Nancy Koc/Adam White, London, UK

DATE OF COMPLETION/PRODUCT LAUNCH: 1988

CLIENT'S BRIEF: Shiseido, the world's third largest cosmetics manufacturer, wanted a package design for a new collection of men's toiletries aimed at the Japanese youth market.

DESIGN RATIONALE: To create an up-to-date image, Pentagram's design incorporated graphic elements found in current Japanese youth culture. A collage combined symbols and letters (based on the brand name "Trendy") with bright day-glow colours. The bottles were given exaggerated, rippled shoulders and brightly coloured plastic triangles extending from the caps. The result reflected the break with tradition found in the Japanese youth movement.

Les Huiles Essentielles

CLIENT: Yves Rocher, Issy Les Moulineaux, France

DESCRIPTION OF PRODUCT: Aromatherapy bath oils

DESIGNER: Lucilla Scrimgeour, Lewis Moberly, London, UK

ILLUSTRATOR: Lucilla Scrimgeour

DATE OF COMPLETION/PRODUCT LAUNCH: December 1989

TARGET MARKET: Young women

PLACE OF SALE: Yves Rocher specialist toiletry shops throughout France

CLIENT'S BRIEF: To design packaging that reflected the natural ethical properties of the oils. In addition, it was important to create a balance between efficacy and beauty.

DESIGN RATIONALE: As a range of aromatherapy oils they required sensitive graphics. The logo is unusual in that it extends right around the elegantly shaped glass bottle and the carton, taking the eye around the form and creating a "tactile" dialogue with the consumer.

Regime

CLIENT: J Sainsbury plc, London, UK

DESCRIPTION OF PRODUCT: A new range of
dermatologically tested skin care products including,
Facial Wash Gel (150ml); Cleansing Milk (200ml);
Alcohol-free Toner (200ml); Daily Moisturising Lotion
(75ml); Daily Moisturising Treatment (50ml) and
Nourishing Night Cream (60ml)

DESIGNER: Lloyd Northover, London, UK

DATE OF COMPLETION/PRODUCT LAUNCH: January 1992

TARGET MARKET: Modern women of 25 years and over
who expect the product to perform well, without having
to pay a premium for it

PLACE OF SALE: Sainsbury's stores

CLIENT'S BRIEF: The personality of the "Regime" brand
should convey premium quality with clear feminine
appeal. Surface pack graphics should be clear and simple
– classic cosmetic packaging. The Regime range
competes on the shelf with other high-quality products
such as L'Oreal "Plénitude".

DESIGN RATIONALE: The clean, fresh, surface graphics
convey an impression of quality and modernity. The gold
sun/moon symbol represents a 24-hour skin care routine,
which is reinforced by numbering the products 1 to 4, to
represent the four steps in this daily regime (1) Cleanse,
(2) Tone, (3) Moisturise (day) and (4) Moisturise (night).

Molto Missoni

CLIENT: Molto Missoni, Orlane, Italy

DESCRIPTION OF PRODUCT: Molto Missoni fragrance for women

DESIGNER: Desgrippes Cato Gobe Group, Paris, France

DATE OF COMPLETION/PRODUCT LAUNCH: 1990

TARGET MARKET: Women with a taste for elegance

PLACE OF SALE: Missoni boutiques, selected perfumeries and duty-free shops

CLIENT'S BRIEF: To create a new women's fragrance for this famous Italian fashion designer.

DESIGN RATIONALE: To make a special niche for this perfume within the famous clothes designer's world of subtle warm colours woven into distinctive, sparkling clothes, an infinite variety of coloured bottles was created.

Boucheron

CLIENT: P.C.I. Boucheron, Paris, France

DESCRIPTION OF PRODUCT: Boucheron women's and men's fragrances

DESIGNER: Desgrippes Cato Gobe Group, Paris, France

DATE OF COMPLETION/PRODUCT LAUNCH: 1988 and 1991

TARGET MARKET: Worldwide

PLACE OF SALE: Boucheron boutiques, selected perfumeries and duty-free shops

CLIENT'S BRIEF: The launch of the first fragrance for the jeweller Alain Boucheron, extending his influence to include top of the line new product ranges.

DESIGN RATIONALE: Creation of the feminine fragrance line was inspired by the famous Boucheron jewellery, carefully preserving the colours and atmosphere of his design. Today the same rationale has been used to create the Boucheron men's fragrance range as well as the Boucheron fragrance boutique. This design was awarded "the best fragrance" in Italy and the USA, the packaging Oscar and Worldstar for packaging in 1989.

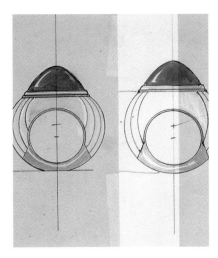

26

Frankincense & Myrrh Range

CLIENT: Czech & Speake Ltd, London, UK

DESCRIPTION OF PRODUCT: Brown boxes, shoulder cases (tubes) and hatboxes with block, oriental-style labels in black and gold

DESIGNER: Czech & Speake Ltd, London, UK

DATE OF COMPLETION/PRODUCT LAUNCH: 1983

TARGET MARKET: This is a male and female fragrance, but in reality, a higher percentage of males use the range. A fragrance for all age groups which is aimed also at the Christmas market and gifts. Males of 25–45, mostly English, American and Italian, purchase the cologne.

PLACE OF SALE: Retail shop and wholesale market in UK, Europe, USA and Japan

CLIENT'S BRIEF: This range was created originally to appeal to the Christmas market, but to also attract both males and females who like an Oriental type of fragrance. The products were also aimed at those wanting a slightly heavier evening fragrance, with spicy and smoky dry notes.

DESIGN RATIONALE: Czech & Speake wanted to create a very Oriental type of packaging, using browns, gold and black. Since brown can look flat as a colour, gold was applied to block labels on the front of the boxes, which also gave the packaging a very Eastern look. The original concept for the labels came from an old wine label, and the idea flourished. The filigree pattern on the hand-drawn foiled labels endorsed the Eastern feel.

Haircare Products

CLIENT: Shiseido, Tokyo, Japan

DESCRIPTION OF PRODUCT: Range of haircare products and toiletries

DESIGNER: Shiseido Design Department, Tokyo, Japan

DATE OF COMPLETION/PRODUCT LAUNCH: 1991

PLACE OF SALE: Professional haircare salons and pharmacies

Boots Haircare Range

CLIENT: Boots Co Ltd, Northampton, UK

PRODUCT: Professional haircare range

DESCRIPTION OF PRODUCT: Shampoo, conditioner, hairspray, mousses and gels, brushes, combs and hairdressing accessories

DESIGNER: Harry Pearce, Newell and Sorrell, London, UK

DATE OF COMPLETION/PRODUCT LAUNCH: July 1989

Delicatessen Foods

CLIENT: Carluccios, London, UK

DESCRIPTION OF PRODUCT: Specially packaged delicatessen foods

DESIGNER: Kontrapunkt, London, UK

DATE OF COMPLETION: October 1991

TARGET MARKET: A, B, C (both sexes)

PLACE OF SALE: Specialist Italian food shop

CLIENT'S BRIEF: To design a brand identity and packaging concept for a modern specialist Italian food shop

DESIGN RATIONALE: A logo which reflects traditional quality. Simple understated packaging using informative and friendly text. Strong branding on all labels.

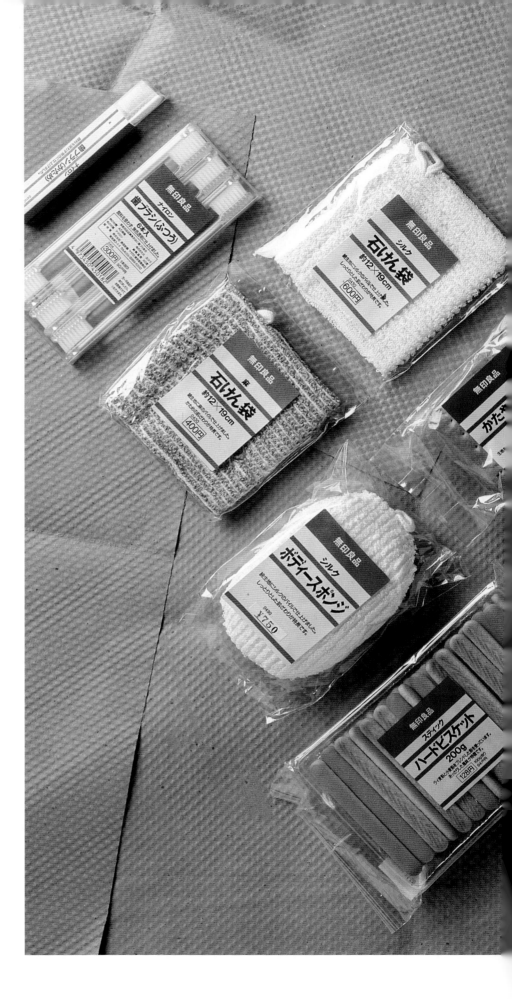

Muji

CLIENT: Mujirushi Ryohin Europe, London, UK

DESIGNER: The Design Department of Ryohin Keikaku
Co Ltd, London, UK

PHOTOGRAPHER: Kulbir Thandi

DATE OF COMPLETION/PRODUCT LAUNCH: 1980

TARGET MARKET: All customers who are interested in
good materials and good quality at the right price.
Aimed at those who rejected the obsession with
expensive designer labels of the early '80s.

PLACE OF SALE: Murirushi Ryohin, Japan. 220 retail
outlets. Mujirushi Ryohin Europe, 3 shops in UK (from
October '92). Muji Hong Kong, 3 shops (from October
'93).

CLIENT'S BRIEF: Muji started in 1980 as an antithesis to
the overpriced, overlabelled consumer products available
in Japan in 1980s. The aim was, and still is, to provide
functional products that are simply designed, and well-
made, using good natural materials with no unnecessary
packaging or designer hype.

DESIGN RATIONALE: The design of the product is to
provide function and simplicity. The concept of the
product comes first, followed by the material, the
ingenuity of manufacture and, finally, a packaging
design to complement material and function without
detracting from either.

Red Band Venco Series

CLIENT: Red Band Venco BV, Breda, The Netherlands

DESCRIPTION OF PRODUCT: A wide range of sweet and liquorice products to come under a single brand. Packaged in a three-sided polypropylene bag

DESIGNER: Eugene Bay/Marcel Gort, Visser Bay Anders Toscani, Amsterdam, The Netherlands

ILLUSTRATION: A. Sidwell, M. Munday, D. Sim, K. O'Brian, C. Porter, P. Tucker, H. Manning, K. O'Keefe, D. Ani, T. Barten, H. McManus, H. Tamba, N. Anderson and R. Slabbers

DATE OF COMPLETION/PRODUCT LAUNCH: January 1990

TARGET MARKET: Mass market

PLACE OF SALE: Supermarkets, sports centres, petrol stations, and so forth

CLIENT'S BRIEF: To create an umbrella brand to cover a wide range of sweets and liquorice products, the link between these products being their natural ingredients. All products in this range were to have one pack size if possible.

DESIGN RATIONALE: Red Band is such a famous brand in the Netherlands that it seemed obvious to use it for this range. The brand logo was used deliberately large on pack, allowing greater freedom for the various illustrations. Each visual was chosen to reflect the different sort of product. The idea of a "collection" was strengthened when all the products were presented together.

Purina Pet Accessories

CLIENT: Gallina Blanca Purina SA, Barcelona, Spain

DESCRIPTION OF PRODUCT: Dog and cat leads

DESIGNER: Addison Design Consultants, London, UK

ILLUSTRATOR/PHOTOGRAPHER: Brian Grimwood

TARGET MARKET: Pet owners

PLACE OF SALE: Shops and supermarkets throughout Spain

CLIENT'S BRIEF: To create a range of pet accessories that built on the existing brand identity and would appeal to pet owners throughout Spain.

DESIGN RATIONALE: To create a full line of accessories with a special merchandizing system. Names were selected, Care, Hobby and Love Chow, that are easily understood in Spanish. Bright and colourful illustrations suggested the pet owner's ideal image of a cat or dog at home: happy and relaxed.

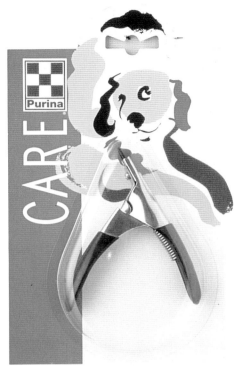

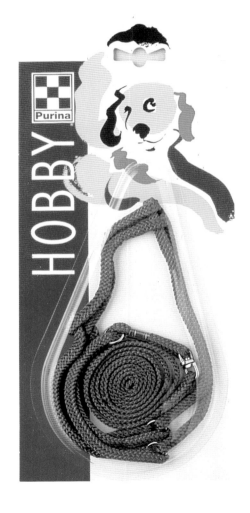

35

Valderma Skin Care Range

CLIENT: Roche Products Ltd, Welwyn Garden City, Herts, UK

DESCRIPTION OF PRODUCT: Range of skincare products

DESIGNER: Minale, Tattersfield & Partners Limited, Richmond, Surrey, UK

DATE OF COMPLETION/PRODUCT LAUNCH: March 1991

TARGET MARKET: Teenagers for the Active Gel; the family for Valderma soap and women for Valderma cream

PLACE OF SALE: Chemists shops and supermarkets

CLIENT'S BRIEF: To strengthen brand loyalty among existing users and to create a strong shelf presence appealing to first-time users.

DESIGN RATIONALE: The new design by Minale Tattersfield uses a triangular slice off the top of the vertical square-sectioned pack to create the "V" of Valderma in contrasting colour. The result is unique both in colour and in shape. The traditional blue (associated with medical skincare products) has been subtly altered with the addition of a touch of green – in combination with a series of contrasting secondary colours: pink for the cream, blue for the soap, bright yellow for the gel and red for the foot cream. The addition of a pharmaceutical "cross" formed by the two "V's" of Valderma adds medical weight.

Ostlers

CLIENT: Lyons Biscuits, Barnsley, S. Yorkshire, UK

DESCRIPTION OF PRODUCT: Biscuit/cake

DESIGNER: Coley Porter Bell, London, UK

DATE OF COMPLETION/PRODUCT LAUNCH: May 1991

PLACE OF SALE: Mass market

CLIENT'S BRIEF: To create a unique brand name, positioning packaging and graphics to support this extraordinary new product which is neither a biscuit nor a cake, but a new kind of snack.

DESIGN RATIONALE: Unique box outer with woodcut graphics. Product name is quirky (supported by quirky advertising launch) and whole design appearance of pack was to stimulate interest.

Speciality Teas

CLIENT: Safeway PLC, Hayes, Middlesex, UK

DESCRIPTION OF PRODUCT: Range of loose and bagged speciality teas

DESIGNER: The Jenkins Group, London, UK

ILLUSTRATOR OR PHOTOGRAPHER: Tim Hill

DATE OF PRODUCT LAUNCH: 1989

PLACE OF SALE: Safeway supermarkets

CLIENT'S BRIEF: To create a range of speciality tea packaging while identifying the individual characteristics of each product. The popular colour associations for each tea blend – for example blue for Assam, grey for Darjeeling – were to be maintained.

DESIGN RATIONALE: Striking still-life photography propped with colour-themed 'objets d'art' create a nostalgic colonial ambience evoking the Victorian occasion of tea drinking. Metallic hues from silver to bronze combine with delicate bone china to emphasize the aspirational nature of fine teas.

Harden & Huyse
Chocolates

CLIENT: Hardenne & Huyse, Saskatoon, Saskatchewan, Canada

DESIGNER: Primo Angeli Inc, San Francisco, CA, USA

DATE OF PRODUCT LAUNCH: February 1992

TARGET MARKET: High-end chocolate consumers

PLACE OF SALE: Good quality retail outlets

CLIENT'S BRIEF: To develop a high-end packaging design programme that establishes Hardenne & Huyse with an international look on the level of an up-scale chocolate company, such as Godiva. Modular container units were developed for display and ease and economics of shipping.

Liz Claiborne for Men

CLIENT: Liz Claiborne Inc, New York, USA

DESCRIPTION OF PRODUCT: Bottle with acid-etched glass, plastic cap, santoprine boot. Box: matte invercote stock, printed and embossed, glossy laminated double flute liner

DESIGNER: Design Director: Ivan Chermayeff; Designers: Ivan Chermayeff, Lorraine Ferguson and Piera Grandesso, Chermayeff & Geismar Inc, New York, USA

PHOTOGRAPHER: Evan Cohen

DATE OF COMPLETION/PRODUCT LAUNCH: September 1989

TARGET MARKET: Men of all ages

PLACE OF SALE: Claiborne is sold in major department stores throughout the USA and Canada, with the potential to enter new markets in the future

CLIENT'S BRIEF: Design of all aspects of packaging for the new men's fragrance. The aim was to break through the competitive clutter by introducing a fragrance and package that is unlike the others, yet is friendly, inviting, and approachable.

DESIGN RATIONALE: The design is black and red; masculine and tactile. A red cube cap and a rubber base that is almost automotive in feeling. The aim was to develop a look by using new materials in new combinations. The look and a feel had to be masculine and strong, and it also had to be dominant in the market place.

Lacoste pour Homme

CLIENT: Lacoste, Paris, France

DESCRIPTION OF PRODUCT: Toiletries for men, including shampoo, eau de toilette, shampoo, deodorant, soap, and shaving materials

DESIGNER: Alain Carré Design Etude, Paris, France

DATE OF COMPLETION/PRODUCT LAUNCH: 1983

TARGET MARKET: For men who are elegant, relaxed and sporty

PLACE OF SALE: Lacoste boutiques and department stores

CLIENT'S BRIEF: To provide an image that would help identify the target market: elegant, relaxed and sporting looking.

DESIGN RATIONALE: The white and green packaging looks cool, the shape and form is compact, the form and colours aim to combine a traditional appeal with a modern look.

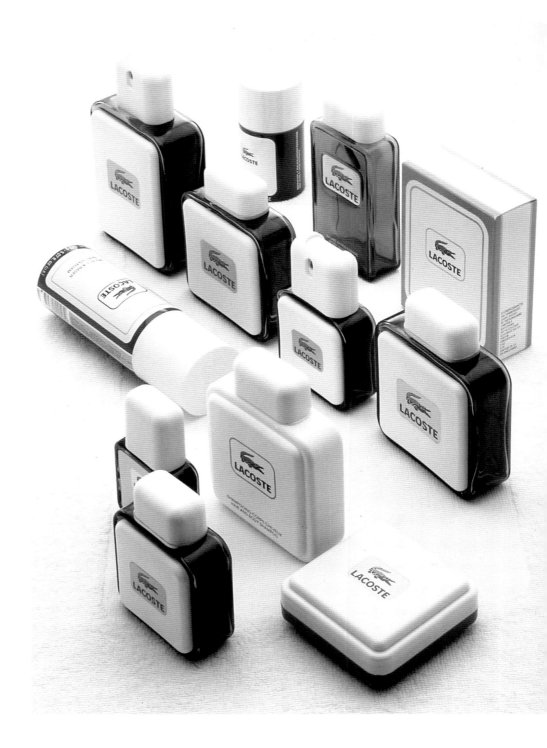

TRIO EYESHADOW   WATER RESISTANT MASCARA   LIPSTICK   PRESSED FACE POWDER

'J' Additions

CLIENT: J Sainsbury PLC, London, UK

DESCRIPTION OF PRODUCT: Range of cosmetics packaged in PVC clam pack outer with card insert

DESIGNER: Coley Porter Bell and Planet Design, London, UK

DATE OF COMPLETION/PRODUCT LAUNCH: March 1990

TARGET MARKET: Sainsbury's customer, female 25–45

PLACE OF SALE: Toiletries aisle, supermarkets

CLIENT'S BRIEF: To launch an added value range of cosmetics to complement the 'J' range from Sainsbury's.

DESIGN RATIONALE: The design was created to add value to the positioning, focusing on skincare benefits.

Eclectic

One of the things that most impresses designers on their first visit to Japan is the care and attention paid by the Japanese to their packaging of presents. In the tradition of Japanese culture, a single flower used in Ikebana becomes a symbol not simply for all flowers but for an entire season. This "microcosm" concept applies also to the tiny gifts or sweets that the Japanese take on every house visit. Boxes of beautifully shaped sweets are wrapped and tied with such care and artistry that Westerners can hardly bring themselves to open them. In effect, the packaging and the care taken over it becomes as important as the contents themselves.

If you buy a small object in an Indian street market, it might be wrapped in rough brown paper or local newsprint, or it might be packed in a box, padded with coconut fibres, tied with rough twine. This is packaging out of tradition and necessity — using whatever you have to hand.

In this chapter, these two influences come together. Many examples are hand-packed by either the manufacturers themselves or by suppliers who buy the products from a variety of sources and then pack them together in a way that creates drama and desirability.

A leaf binds a few sheets of notepaper together, some seashells and seedpods add an extra dimension to soaps and bathsalts, and fibre plant pots are recruited to contain chillis and cinnamon sticks. This form of packaging engages the emotional responses we feel towards hand-made gifts and natural objects and appeals to the sophisticated eye. They lock into a trend for the eclectic, and they strike a sharp contrast to the impersonal world of mass-production.

Gift Boxes

CLIENT: Nomades Authentic, Villemomble, France

DESCRIPTION OF PRODUCT: Recycled cardboard and
natural materials

DESIGNER: Nomades Authentic, Villemomble, France

DATE OF COMPLETION/PRODUCT LAUNCH: January 1990

TARGET MARKET: Present buyers

PLACE OF SALE: Gift shops and general stores

DESIGN RATIONALE: We love natural materials and
would like to communicate this love to other people.

Stationery Sets

CLIENT: Nomades Authentic, Villemomble, France

DESCRIPTION OF PRODUCT: Recycled cardboard and
paper, and natural materials

DATE OF COMPLETION/PRODUCT LAUNCH: January 1990

TARGET MARKET: Present buyers

PLACE OF SALE: Gift shops and general stores

Bath Salts and Soaps

CLIENT: Nomades Authentic, Villemomble, France

DESCRIPTION OF PRODUCT: Recycled cardboard and natural materials

DESIGNER: Nomades Authentic, Villemomble, France

DATE OF COMPLETION/PRODUCT LAUNCH: January 1990

TARGET MARKET: Present buyers

PLACE OF SALE: Gift shops and general stores

Honey and Preserves

CLIENT: Nomades Authentic, Villemomble, France

DESCRIPTION OF PRODUCT: Recycled cardboard and paper, and natural materials

DATE OF COMPLETION/PRODUCT LAUNCH: January 1990

TARGET MARKET: Present buyers

PLACE OF SALE: Gift shops and general stores

Fagots d'Encens

CLIENT: Miller et Bertaux, Paris, France

DESCRIPTION OF PRODUCT: Incense sticks (40cm long) tied with a lotus leaf and papyrus, with a cotton ribbon

DESIGNER: Miller et Bertaux, Paris, France

DATE OF COMPLETION/PRODUCT LAUNCH: October 1991

PLACE OF SALE: Miller et Bertaux boutiques

DESIGN RATIONALE: For Miller et Bertaux the packaging has a symbolic value that accords with the care and quality brought to the manufacture of the product.

Composition Blanche

CLIENT: Miller et Bertaux, Paris, France

DESIGNER: Miller et Bertaux, Paris, France

DATE OF COMPLETION/PRODUCT LAUNCH: October 1991

PLACE OF SALE: Miller et Bertaux boutiques

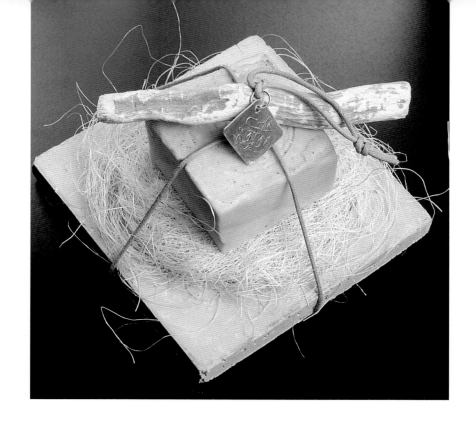

Three cloths

CLIENT: Miller et Bertaux, Paris, France

DESCRIPTION OF PRODUCT: Each cloth is in Egyptian cotton; size 50 x 76cm

DESIGNER: Miller et Bertaux, Paris, France

DATE OF COMPLETION/PRODUCT LAUNCH: October 1991

PLACE OF SALE: Miller et Bertaux boutiques

Cèdre

CLIENT: Miller et Bertaux, Paris, France

DESIGNER: Miller et Bertaux, Paris, France

DATE OF COMPLETION/PRODUCT LAUNCH: September 1990

PLACE OF SALE: Miller et Bertaux boutiques

Coffret Hammam

CLIENT: Miller et Bertaux, Paris, France

DESIGNER: Miller et Bertaux, Paris, France

DATE OF COMPLETION/PRODUCT LAUNCH: September 1990

PLACE OF SALE: Miller et Bertaux boutiques

Seashore Range

CLIENT: The Conran Shop, London, UK

DESCRIPTION OF PRODUCT: Bath toiletries range

DESIGNER: Robert Thorburn, Albion Botanicals, Cambridge, UK

DATE OF COMPLETION/PRODUCT LAUNCH: 1991

TARGET MARKET: Adult customers, male and female

PLACE OF SALE: The Conran Shop, London, UK

Potpourri

CLIENT: The Conran Shop, London, UK and Liberty's of Regent Street, London, UK

DESCRIPTION OF PRODUCT: Wrapped boxes, folded papers and packets tied with raffia, ribbon or string

DESIGNER: Nicola Lesbird at the Conran Shop in London, UK, in conjunction with Robert Thorburn at Albion Botanicals, London, UK, Helen Pett/Albion Botanicals and others

DATE OF COMPLETION/PRODUCT LAUNCH: 1991

TARGET MARKET: Gift customers

PLACE OF SALE: Products exclusive to the Conran Shop (retail store in London selling very high-quality and design led products) or Liberty's of Regent Street

CLIENT'S BRIEF: No brief was given, the product was worked on as a joint effort, led by Nicola Lesbird, then of Conran Shop buying team, for the Conran Shop products

DESIGN RATIONALE: To design a new generation of potpourri to suit the style of The Conran Shop and Liberty's, and their customers.

Range of Stationery

CLIENT: Printed Matter Ltd, London, UK

DESCRIPTION OF PRODUCT: Hand-made, ecologically sound recycled stationery – writing paper, envelopes, blotters, cards, tags etc. in gift sets

DESIGNER: Beth Nelson, Printed Matter (London) Ltd, London, UK

DATE OF COMPLETION/PRODUCT LAUNCH: 1991/1992

TARGET MARKET: UK and international high-end giftware and stationery markets

PLACE OF SALE: The Conran Shop, London; Neiman Marcus, USA

DESIGN RATIONALE: This range of stationery was devised in 1989 with the aim of producing hand-made, ecologically sound products

Thomas the Tank Engine Gift Set

CLIENT: The Boots Company, Nottingham, UK

DESIGNER: Andrew Lane, Grosvenor of London PLC, London, UK

DATE OF COMPLETION/PRODUCT LAUNCH: 1992

DESIGN RATIONALE: To create a design concept that would appeal to both children and parents, and to ensure that the product encouraged children to clean their teeth.

Natural Collection Gift Baskets

CLIENT: The Boots Company, Nottingham, UK

DESIGNER: Smith & Milton, London, W1

DATE OF COMPLETION/PRODUCT LAUNCH: 1988/9

TARGET MARKET: Women aged 15–25 years

PLACE OF SALE: Boots retail outlets

Laurel

CLIENT: Mark Salkild/Fiona Barclay, Laurel, Ruddington, Nottinghamshire, UK

DESCRIPTION OF PRODUCT: A collection of gifts comprising napkins, candles, games, stationery, herbs and soaps contained in individual wooden boxes and handmade and decorated in the UK

DESIGNER: Laurel, Ruddington, Nottinghamshire, UK

PHOTOGRAPHER: Terry Cotterill

DATE OF COMPLETION/PRODUCT LAUNCH: April 1992

TARGET MARKET: Retail gift-shop outlets/interior designers

PLACE OF SALE: As above (UK or export)

CLIENT'S BRIEF: Boxes are made up from renewable wood (Douglas Fir with a rough finish to complement the decoration).

DESIGN RAATIONALE: The box is not a throwaway item after the contents have been used; therefore there is no distinction between the packaging and its contents.

Shoe Care

CLIENT: The Silver Crane Company, Bournemouth, Dorset, UK

DESCRIPTION OF PRODUCT: 7in round tin with contents

DESIGNER: Peter Hobbs Design Associates, Richmond, Surrey, UK

ILLUSTRATOR: Peter Hobbs

DATE OF COMPLETION/PRODUCT LAUNCH: 1985/86

TARGET MARKET: Gift shops clientèle

PLACE OF SALE: Gift shops

Prestigious

Luxury packaging is synonymous with luxury products. Havana cigars in a beautiful wooden box or a canteen of cutlery in a velvet-lined case sealed with a brass catch exude an air of fine quality and tradition. The projects in this chapter have adopted many of these same qualities: hand-crafted manufacture, intricately detailed graphics and traditional materials. By contrasting materials, such as glass packed in wood, by using rich colours with gold or silver, and by "over" packaging — jeans in a miniature cardboard suitcase with a handle, or socks in perfectly proportioned cardboard sleeve boxes — manufacturers can give special prestige values to otherwise somewhat mundane merchandise.

Ty Nant Original Spring Water

CLIENT: Ty Nant Spring Water Limited, Lampeter, Dyfed, Wales

DESCRIPTION OF PRODUCT: Ty Nant Original Spring Water is produced in distinctive blue glass bottles, sizes 750ml, 330ml and 250ml, and available in still or softly carbonated versions

DESIGNER: Ty Nant Spring Water Limited, Lampeter, Dyfed, Wales

DATE OF PRODUCT LAUNCH: November 1989

TARGET MARKET: Hotel, restaurant, catering, leisure and licensed trades

PLACE OF SALE: As above, and off licences, supermarkets etc, in UK and abroad

CLIENT'S BRIEF: A premium spring water. Ty Nant Original is sourced from an underground aquifer, beneath the Welsh Cambrian mountains. Available worldwide, Ty Nant has filled a niche in the market for beautifully presented, natural spring water where quality is of paramount importance.

DESIGN RATIONALE: Ty Nant Original was designed to complement all table settings. So successful is the design concept that Ty Nant is now considered to be the market leader for premium bottled spring water. Winner of the 1989 British Glass "First Glass" award for design excellence.

Lutz

CLIENT: Holsten Distributors, London, UK

DESCRIPTION OF PRODUCT: Dry beer – bottled

DESIGNER: Coley Porter Bell, London, UK

DATE OF COMPLETION/PRODUCT LAUNCH: 1991

PLACE OF SALE: Bars

CLIENT'S BRIEF: To create a new brand for Holsten distributors, extending their portfolio beyond Holsten Pils. Although the product is a "dry" beer, the objective was to create a broader market for the new brand than for other dry beers.

DESIGN RATIONALE: To create a central brand marque around a name with good "bar call". Bottle colour conveys refreshment values while design communicates simplicity and authenticity. The approach avoids the trap of over-designing.

Aspects

CLIENT: T. G. Smith (Fine Foods) Ltd, Bootle, Lancashire, UK

DESCRIPTION OF PRODUCT: 125g and 150g cartons

DESIGNER: Chris Abrahams, Light & Coley Ltd, London UK

ILLUSTRATOR OR PHOTOGRAPHER: Chris Abrahams and Brem Bremner

DATE OF COMPLETION/PRODUCT LAUNCH: Spring 1991

TARGET MARKET: Upper range, principally female

PLACE OF SALE: Grocery multiples, confectionery specialists

CLIENT'S BRIEF: To develop name, pack construction and graphics for a range of coated nut and fruit confectionery products at the luxury end of the market.

DESIGN RATIONALE: In order to meet the product positioning and communicate the lavish and elegant product proposition, Light & Coley developed an aspirational name, clean typography, inviting representation of the product and "high fashion" lifestyle illustrations.

Seppelt 100-Year-Old Para Liqueur

CLIENT: B. Seppelt & Sons Ltd, Adelaide, South Australia

DESCRIPTION OF PRODUCT: 100-year-old port wine presented in a specially designed and made Italian bottle, together with the wine's Certificate of Authentication in a hand-made velvet-lined walnut presentation case. The bottle is hand-labelled.

DESIGNER: Barrie Tucker, Barrie Tucker Design Pty Ltd, Eastwood, South Australia

DATE OF COMPLETION/PRODUCT LAUNCH: October 1990

TARGET MARKET: International wine collectors and connoisseurs

PLACE OF SALE: Available direct only from B. Seppelt & Sons, South Australia. Orders are placed via their international agents and representatives

CLIENT'S BRIEF: To repackage this very special wine. B. Seppelt & Sons is the only wine company in the world with stocks of over 100 vintages of fortified wine, enabling the company to release 100-year-old Para Liqueur each year since 1978. Para Liqueur, regarded internationally as a collector's item, retails at approximately US$2,000 per bottle.

DESIGN RATIONALE: A product such as this, which is rare in the world, deserved the development of its own unique packaging. Barrie Tucker reacted by designing a bottle of which only 500 were produced by a specialist Italian glass maker.

Angove's Winemakers Limited Edition

CLIENT: Angove's Pty Ltd, Renmark, Australia

DESCRIPTION OF PRODUCT: Limited release Chardonnay and Cabernet Sauvignon, packaged in a 750ml bottle and 6-bottle carton

DESIGNER: Barrie Tucker, Barrie Tucker Design Pty Ltd, Eastwood, South Australia

DATE OF COMPLETION/PRODUCT LAUNCH: October 1990

PLACE OF SALE: Bottle shops and restaurants in Australia

CLIENT'S BRIEF: Established in 1886, Angove's is one of Australia's largest remaining family-owned wine and brandy companies. The wines in this range were "hand-made" in the literal sense, and because of the production methods employed, were produced in extremely limited quantities. The packaging design reflects the unique and distinctive quality of the wines.

DESIGN RATIONALE: The image on the label depicts Barrie Tucker's idea of the wine's origins.

Vichy Pastilles

CLIENT: Warner Lambert Group – Parke Davis, France

DESCRIPTION OF PRODUCT: Vichy Pastilles

DESIGNER: Desgrippes Cato Gobe Group, Paris, France

DATE OF COMPLETION/PRODUCT LAUNCH: 1990

PLACE OF SALE: Supermarkets, candy counters and pharmacies (a different package design for the mass market and the pharmacies respectively)

CLIENT'S BRIEF: After buying the brand to help the company impinge on the French market, Warner Lambert decided to update the image of the famous product.

DESIGN RATIONALE: This was an elaboration of the brand's advertising concept. "The pleasure of well-being" together with a definition of the new name: "Vichy Pastilles Source". A design of the new brand identity was also needed together with a graphic creation for the decor of each element in the range. A definition of the new "Vichy Forme", sugar-free range was needed as was the graphic creation of "Vichy Forme" sugar-free packaging.

Beauté Capillaire

CLIENT: Carita, Paris, France

DESCRIPTION OF PRODUCT: Half-moon shape plastic
bottle with a service cap (150 × 75 × 20mm)

DESIGNER: Thierry Lecoule Design, Paris, France

ILLUSTRATOR/PHOTOGRAPHER: Christophe Tournebize

DATE OF COMPLETION/PRODUCT LAUNCH: 1990

TARGET MARKET: All women

PLACE OF SALE: Selective perfumeries and Carita
Institutes

CLIENT'S BRIEF: No specific brief was given to Thierry
Lecoule for this creation.

DESIGN RATIONALE: On the basis of the cardboard
packaging, Thierry Lecoule did propose on his own
initiative to create a specific shape which would perfectly
match with Carita's brand image. This is how a new and
contemporary shape was created whose original and
pure lines were matched by a high level of technical
realization.

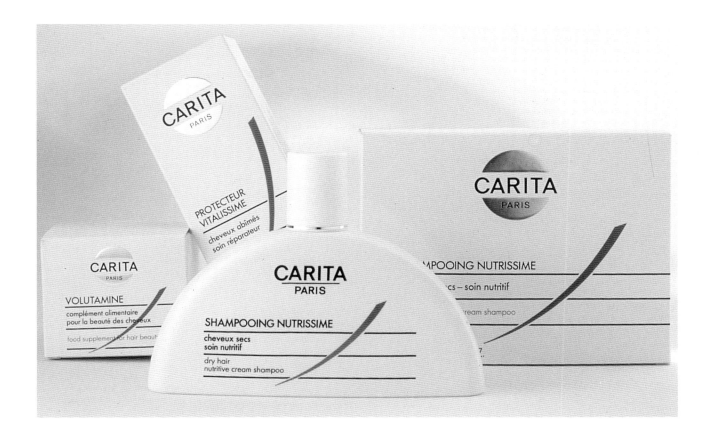

Chocolates Valrhona

CLIENT: Valrhona, Tain L'Hermitage, France

DESCRIPTION OF PRODUCT: A metallic box for the packaging with a black background, underlined by red and gold

DESIGNER: MBD Design, Bagnolet, France

DATE OF COMPLETION/PRODUCT LAUNCH: Guanaja: 1987; Caraibes: 1990

TARGET MARKET: General public

PLACE OF SALE: Baker's shops, patisseries, confectioners

CLIENT'S BRIEF: Valrhona, a leading French chocolate manufacturer traditionally specializing in chocolate "covering" of raw material for confectioners and pastrymakers, launched a major plan for repositioning its brand name and for creating new products aimed at the general public.

DESIGN RATIONALE: To create new packaging and a new image symbol of high-quality chocolate. Red, black and gold were chosen for the luxury connotation, and the metallic box for the precious product image. The design task went further, recreating the professional environment of chocolate. Inside the box is a card recounting the history of cacao (the basis of chocolate) since its discovery in 1502 by Christopher Columbus.

Linden Lady Chocolates

CLIENT: Linden Lady Chocolates, Colchester, Essex, UK

DESCRIPTION OF PRODUCT: Handmade chocolates

DESIGNER: Mary Lewis, Lewis Moberly, London, UK

PHOTOGRAPHER: Alan David Tu

ILLUSTRATOR: Andrew McNab

DATE OF COMPLETION/PRODUCT LAUNCH: December 1988

TARGET MARKET: Discerning chocoholics

PLACE OF SALE: Specialist confectioners and quality stores

CLIENT'S BRIEF: To design a corporate identity, packaging form and graphics that would reflect the quality of these exquisite handmade chocolates.

DESIGN RATIONALE: The peacock is a symbol of the Linden Lady legend and is the theme of the identity and packaging. Set in the centre of the chocolates is a tiny box containing one single chocolate, the "Secret Lady". A leaflet explains the Linden Lady legend.

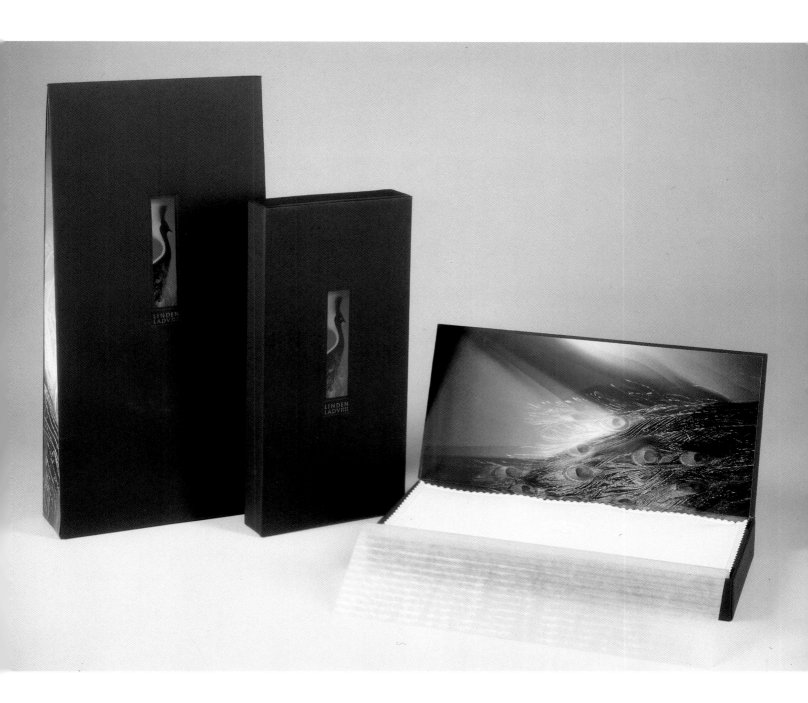

Cutty Sark 12 yr (Scotch Whisky)

CLIENT: Berry Bros & Rudd, London, UK

DESCRIPTION OF PRODUCT: Ten-sided bottle (750ml) containing whisky, with carton

DESIGNER: John Blackburn, Blackburn's, London, UK

ILLUSTRATOR: Jean Paul Tibbles

TARGET MARKET: Japanese gift market

PLACE OF SALE: Japanese department stores

CLIENT'S BRIEF: To revitalize the brand, and to improve perceived quality and value. It also had to be attractive, stylish and eye catching, and to communicate that this product is part of the "Cutty Sark" brand portfolio

DESIGN RATIONALE: To make the design relevant to the Cutty Sark story and heritage. The bottle and carton are coloured green, which conjures up images of the sea, and creates a visual point of difference in a crowded market.

Glencadam 25-year-old Highland Malt Whisky

CLIENT: Stewart & Son of Dundee Ltd, Dundee, Scotland

DESCRIPTION OF PRODUCT: Limited edition lead-free crystal decanter and presentation box

DESIGNER: Graphic Partners, Edinburgh, Scotland

DATE OF COMPLETION/PRODUCT LAUNCH: 1989

TARGET MARKET: Top of the range Japanese market for Scotch whisky gift decanters

PLACE OF SALE: Japanese specialist gift shops

CLIENT'S BRIEF: Glencadam is an entirely new product that required quality branding and packaging, including the design of the decanter and the box for a top-of-the-range single malt whisky.

DESIGN RATIONALE: The decanter and stopper in special lead-free crystal were hand-cut, ground and polished using traditional methods. The branding was permanently fired onto the crystal in a white gold finish. The lettering is sand-blasted through the white gold using a new technique. The presentation box is a unique construction with an inner display pedestal.

Old Parr Elizabethan Whisky

CLIENT: United Distillers, London, UK

DESCRIPTION OF PRODUCT: Bottle of whisky in a hand-blown crystal decanter, with cotton twist running through it. Pewter portrait frames on sides contain miniature paintings

DESIGNER: John Blackburn, Blackburn's Ltd, London, UK

ILLUSTRATOR: Warren Madill

TARGET MARKET: Japanese corporate gift market

PLACE OF SALE: Duty-free shops and outlets

CLIENT'S BRIEF: To develop the most prestigious Scotch whisky presentation in the world, to rival the most expensive cognacs in the Japanese corporate gift market.

DESIGN RATIONALE: Blackburn's had already designed "Old Parr 12yrs" – the biggest-selling imported brand in Japan. The brand concept is based upon Thomas Parr, England's reputed oldest man, who lived to 152 years. Parr lived through the Tudor era and the design is a celebration of Elizabethan times.

Two Proposed Ranges of Perfume

CLIENT: The Crown Perfumery Company, Ellon, Aberdeenshire, Scotland

DESCRIPTION OF PRODUCT: Prospectus and prototype packaging

DESIGNER: Graphic Partners, Edinburgh, Scotland

DATE OF COMPLETION/PRODUCT LAUNCH: 1989/90

CLIENT'S BRIEF: To create a brand identity and prototype packaging for two proposed perfume ranges.

DESIGN RATIONALE: To give the ranges a strong brand identity and high brand positioning.

Safari Climate Response Body Lotion

CLIENT: Ralph Lauren Fragrances, New York, USA

DESCRIPTION OF PRODUCT: 8.4oz PET faceted plastic bottle, with custom pump

DESIGNER: Ralph Lauren, New York, USA

DATE OF COMPLETION/PRODUCT LAUNCH: March 1991

TARGET MARKET: Women, 25–49 years old

PLACE OF SALE: Department stores. Especially stores in USA, Canada and England

DESIGN RATIONALE: To nterpret fragrance packaging, as closely as possible with faceting, yet provide convenience of pump, in a plastic material.

Safari Parfum

CLIENT: Ralph Lauren Fragrances, New York, USA

DESCRIPTION OF PRODUCT: Safari parfum housed in cut-glass bottle with tear-drop well for product; silver-plated filigree hinged cap, with fake tortoiseshell inlay. Cut-crystal stopper

Own-label Indian & China Tea

CLIENT: Marks & Spencer, London, UK

DESCRIPTION OF PRODUCT: Boxed tea bags and loose packaged tea

DESIGNER: Graphics – Salvatore Cicero, Worthington & Co, London, UK

DATE OF COMPLETION/PRODUCT LAUNCH: 1987

TARGET MARKET: Marks & Spencer's customers

PLACE OF SALE: Marks & Spencer's multiple outlets in UK and France

CLIENT'S BRIEF: To produce a high-quality image – initially for loose tea and subsequently for tea bags.

DESIGN RATIONALE: An authentic look and quality design was produced to promote a premium-priced product of appeal to a demanding and particular clientèle in the UK and France.

Campagnia dell'Arabica

CLIENT: D & C Bologna, Italy

DESCRIPTION OF PRODUCT: Specialist pure Arabica coffee

DESIGNER: Maurizio di Robilant, Milan, Italy

DATE OF COMPLETION/PRODUCT LAUNCH: 1991/2

DESIGN RATIONALE: To produce a suitable packaging concept for a high-end commodity. Colombia coffee is pure, unblended, Arabica coffee. There was no campaign backing for the product – the design of the packaging alone had to situate the coffee in the specialist, luxury end of the market.

Ridley's Jars

CLIENT: Ridley's Country Chandlers, Great Dunmow, Essex, UK

DESCRIPTION OF PRODUCT: Fine-quality preserves, marmalades and savouries in 8oz hexagonal jars and attractive packaging

DESIGNER: As above

DATE OF COMPLETION/PRODUCT LAUNCH: Launched on various dates, starting from 1987 to the present time

TARGET MARKET: Independent shops

PLACE OF SALE: Specialist outlets such as HM Tower of London, the Royal Horticultural Society shop at Wisley and John Lewis department stores

CLIENT'S BRIEF: The Essex countryside is the inspiration for this range. The ever-growing range of "Country Eatables" extends to more than 60 products, plus gift packs, teas and confectionery.

DESIGN RATIONALE: The "Emily Ridley" theme was based on actual places and people found in and around Ridley's, the Essex Brewery which started brewing in Victorian times. The fruits used in our old English recipes would have been gathered from the hedgerows surrounding the brewery and turned into preserves by Emily Ridley herself.

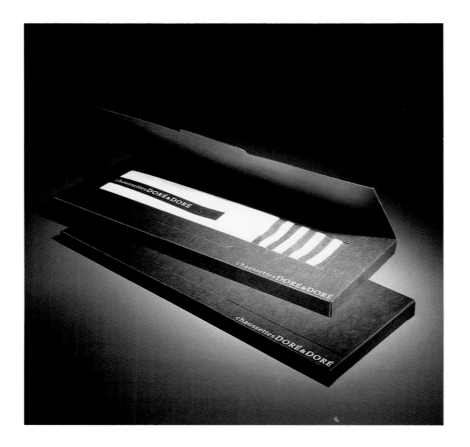

Doré & Doré

CLIENT: Doré-Doré, Mery sur Seine, France

DESCRIPTION OF PRODUCT: Men's socks

DESIGNER: Bob Adamski, Paris, France

ILLUSTRATOR OR PHOTOGRAPHER: Andrew Bettles:
Visual of feet

DATE OF COMPLETION/PRODUCT LAUNCH: 1991

TARGET MARKET: Luxury accessory market

PLACE OF SALE: Specialized men's boutiques and top
market department stores

CLIENT'S BRIEF: The creation of a new label for a luxury
line of men's socks destined for the European market.

DESIGN RATIONALE: The label "Doré & Doré"
reinstalled the company's name (founded in 1890), and
therefore also the product's credibility; the classicism of
the logo and the minimalism of the packaging reinforce
the notion of "quality for the élite".

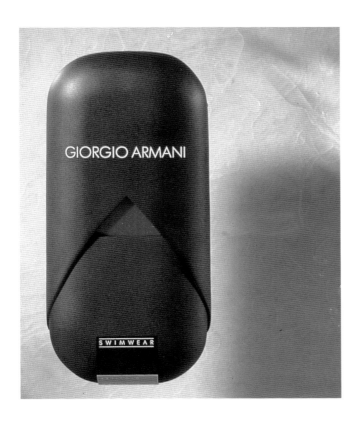

Giorgio Armani

CLIENT: Giorgio Armani Spa, Milan, Italy

DESCRIPTION OF PRODUCT: Packaging for swimwear and underwear

DESIGNER: Minale, Tattersfield & Partners Limited, Richmond, Surrey, UK

DATE OF COMPLETION/PRODUCT LAUNCH: Spring 1986

TARGET MARKET: Men and women in the 18–50 age range

PLACE OF SALE: Throughout the world, especially in Armani shops and concessions in Europe

CLIENT'S BRIEF: The brief was to design packaging for a new range of swimwear and underwear. It also had to sum up the name of Giorgio Armani – renowned for Italian high fashion, design and style.

DESIGN RATIONALE: The resulting packs that Minale Tattersfield designed for Giorgio Armani are highly imaginative and practical; each box has understated graphics in two parts, sliding together to form the letter A (for Armani). The swimwear packaging in particular subscribes to the concept that the best ideas are often the simplest: it is water-resistant, pocket-sized and made of high-impact polystyrene.

Best Direction Jeans

CLIENT: Best Direction Ltd, Greenford, Middlesex, UK

DESCRIPTION OF PRODUCT: Cardboard suitcase with cord handle, containing a pair of jeans with a card insert for accessories

DESIGNER: Big Active Ltd, London, UK

DATE OF COMPLETION/PRODUCT LAUNCH: 1989

TARGET MARKET: Males aged 20 to 40

PLACE OF SALE: High Street fashion retail stores

CLIENT'S BRIEF: To design a special limited edition item

that would contain and display a pair of Best Direction jeans and its accessories, such as belt, shaving kit, spare buttons and labels. This item would be given to particular retail customers to be used as in-store promotion for the brand.

DESIGN RATIONALE: The Best Direction packaging was based on a travel theme, evoking a mood of internationalism. The aim was to design a container for the jeans, the suitcase tied in with the idea of travel.

Rose Range Fragrance

CLIENT: Czech & Speake Ltd, London, UK

DESCRIPTION OF PRODUCT: Classic moiré boxes and shoulder cases (tubes) of silver on pink

DESIGNER: Czech & Speake Ltd, London, UK

DATE OF COMPLETION/PRODUCT LAUNCH: 1985

TARGET MARKET: Women of all ages, particularly those of 25 years and over who are cosmopolitan, sophisticated, elegant and international, and who enjoy the subtlety of an English fine fragrance

PLACE OF SALE: Retail shop and wholesale market in UK, Europe, USA and Japan

CLIENT'S BRIEF: Czech & Speake wanted to develop a fragrance that catered for a wide female age range. It had to be a light, elegant fragrance, not heavy and overpoweringly sweet, as was the case with other rose fragrances on the market. The brief was to create a quintessentially English fragrance, with traditional, understated packaging that was both classic and feminine.

DESIGN RATIONALE: Czech & Speake wanted to create simple, classic lines to its packaging concept. The emphasis was on simplicity. Calling the fragrance simply "Rose" was a deliberately unpretentious stance, and the company wanted this reflected in the packaging and in the elegant "English" feel. The hand-drawn foil blocking on the front of the boxes is simple in design. The moiré silk look was created from wood bark, photographed and then reproduced onto paper with a textured feel. The aim of the packaging was also to create a range of attractively presented toiletries that could be given as gifts for all occasions.

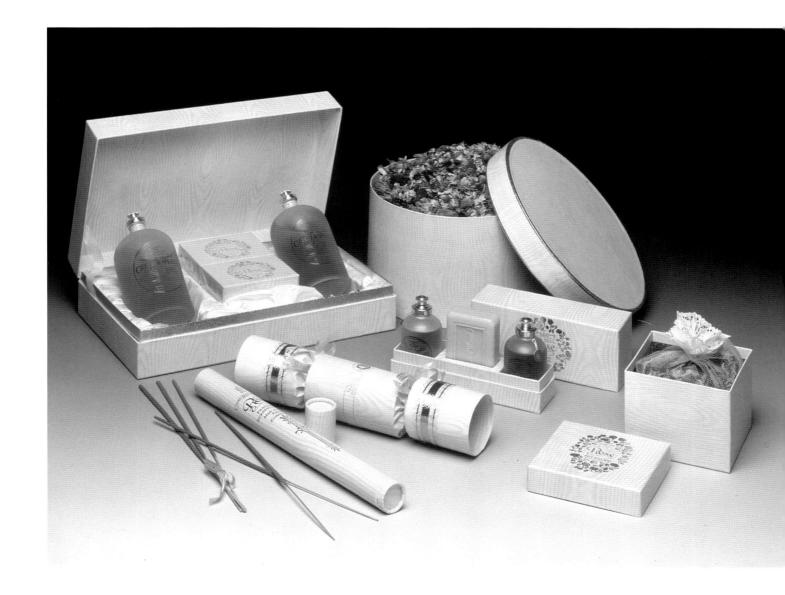

No 88

CLIENT: Czech & Speake Ltd, London, UK

DESCRIPTION OF PRODUCT: Range of hair care/cosmetics

DESIGNER: Czech & Speake Ltd, London, UK

DATE OF COMPLETION/PRODUCT LAUNCH: 1982

TARGET MARKET: International, sophisticated male

PLACE OF SALE: Our own retail outlets, wholesale and overseas outlets and USA

CLIENT'S BRIEF: To create an unusual image for the new range to distinguish it from competitors, and to make it difficult to imitate.

DESIGN RATIONALE: To create a simple but effective design, with subtle packaging. The outer packaging complements the rigid tube of the bottles and gives harmony and flow to the general appearance.

Sensual

Most perfume manufacturers producing up-market products enlist elements of sensuality in their presentation and their packaging. Sometimes it can be more overt than others. Salvador Dali's lips, for Laguna, seem to be literally sections of the female form. At other times, bottles appear to have been moulded like clay rather than designed on paper, and they represent an astonishing amount of background briefing and research. To take one example, the French packaging company, Ateliers Dinand, whose 20 designers work internationally for most of the large perfume manufacturers, often receives a very comprehensive brief. If the client is a fashion house, the brief might include a video as well as details of the customer's profile, market analysis, image of the corporation, target price (of the bottle) and, of course, the qualities of the scent. These qualities might be visualized by photographs of key elements (herbs, plants, landscapes, etc) as well as key words.

Even though the designers start working in sketch form, these sketches will only be used for initial internal discussions. By the time the client sees them, the final four to six (selected from an initial 20 or more) will be modelled full-size (to 30ml or 50ml size bottles) in plexiglass. It is important that the client can get the feel of the bottle, see how the light plays on it, and through it, and how reflections affect it, and how it feels in the hand. So the bottles are developed, carved like a piece of sculpture, by the same designer who conceived the form.

Although computer-aided design has had an enormous impact on the way product designers work — particularly when visualizing shapes in 3D, Dinand feel that the medium is flat and lifeless — more suitable to working on the carton than the bottle.

Their experience working with bottle-makers means that the designer often knows while he or she is working on a shape whether it can be made or not, even if later on he or she has to push the manufacturer to produce it. It is this attention to detail that determines the success, or otherwise, of the final product in design terms.

Hydra Puissance

CLIENT: Yves Rocher, Issy les Moulineaux, France

DESCRIPTION OF PRODUCT: Moisturizer in a glass bottle
with a plastic cap

DESIGNER: Vitrac Design Strategy, Paris, France

DATE OF PRODUCT LAUNCH: 1989

TARGET MARKET: Females for skincare range –
moisturizers

PLACE OF SALE: Mail order and in Yves Rocher boutiques

CLIENT'S BRIEF: The bottle had to put over the
moisturizing qualities of the product.

DESIGN RATIONALE: Pure design with very translucent
materials helps to express the nature of the product.

Noevir 95

CLIENT: Noevir, Milan, Italy

DESCRIPTION OF PRODUCT: Skincare products: cream
jars 30g and 100g; bottles 100ml and 150ml

DESIGNER: Dieter Bakic Design, Milan, Italy

PHOTOGRAPHER: Tronconi, Milan, Italy

DATE OF PRODUCT LAUNCH: November 1990

TARGET MARKET: Japanese luxury market

Andrélon Shampoo

CLIENT: Andrélon Cosmetics, Bodegraven, The
Netherlands

DESCRIPTION OF PRODUCT: Product line of five different
hair treatment shampoos

DESIGNER: Stadium Design, Hillegom, The Netherlands

DATE OF COMPLETION/PRODUCT LAUNCH: Spring 1992

PLACE OF SALE: Supermarkets and drugstores

CLIENT'S BRIEF: To develop next to a line of five basic
shampoos a line of five treatment shampoos that deal
with specific hair problems.

DESIGN RATIONALE: Each shampoo is colour-coded, the
same colours are used in different Andrélon products
that deal with the same hair problems.

Essentials

CLIENT: John Lewis Partnership, London, UK

DESCRIPTION OF PRODUCT: An "own brand" range of toiletries for skin, hair, bath. Bottles 75ml and 150ml (PVC); bottle caps (ABSK resin). Label material: vinyl

DESIGNER: Morrison Dalley Design Partnership, London, UK

ILLUSTRATOR: Helen Cowcher

DATE OF COMPLETION/PRODUCT LAUNCH: Christmas 1989

TARGET MARKET: John Lewis customer – female 25+, interested in "natural" products. Priced for repeat purchase

PLACE OF SALE: John Lewis Partnership stores

CLIENT'S BRIEF: The products were formulated using only pure, natural extracts from plants, fruits and flowers. The design had to reflect this and it also had to develop a stoppered bottle shape.

DESIGN RATIONALE: An appropriate and authentic botanical feel was established by the commissioning of botanical illustrations for each label. This approach was also enhanced by using the original stoppered bottle shape and carried through in the typography and label shapes.

Solea Colotion

CLIENT: Nivea Kao Corporation, Tokyo, Japan

DESCRIPTION OF PRODUCT: The materials are resin. The capacity is 230ml

DESIGNER: Taku Satoh, Tokyo, Japan

DATE OF PRODUCT LAUNCH: May 1987

TARGET MARKET: People who lives in cities

PLACE OF SALE: Throughout Japan

CLIENT'S BRIEF: To create a pack for an economical and fresh-smelling lotion that can be used after a shower on the entire body

DESIGN RATIONALE: The cap, which expresses the design, organically expands on the contents.

Max Factor Moisturemint, Max Factor Toning Mint

CLIENT: Max Factor, Tokyo, Japan

DESCRIPTION OF PRODUCT: The materials are glass and resin with a paper label. The capacities are: Moisture Mint 120ml; Toning Mint 150ml; Cleansing Mint 100g

DESIGNER: Taku Satoh, Tokyo, Japan

DATE OF PRODUCT LAUNCH: May 1987

TARGET MARKET: Adult women

PLACE OF SALE: Throughout Japan

CLIENT'S BRIEF: To create a fashionable and economical skincare series that will be sold in a basket at the front of the shop.

DESIGN RATIONALE: The product's impact is through form rather than through graphic treatment. The caps are made to impress.

FEC Series

CLIENT: Max Factor, Tokyo, Japan

DESCRIPTION OF PRODUCT: The materials are glass, resin and aluminium with a paper label. Face make up formula: 25ml. Lip material: top and bottom 81mm × diameter 15mm. Fluid colours: 25ml. Gradation eyes: top and bottom 77.5mm × right and left 10mm × depth 17.5mm

DESIGNER: Taku Satoh, Tokyo, Japan

DATE OF PRODUCT LAUNCH: October 1986

TARGET MARKET: City-dwelling women who have strong personal opinions

PLACE OF SALE: Throughout Japan

CLIENT'S BRIEF: To present a new urban make-up series for women.

DESIGN RATIONALE: Aluminium has the image of a cold metal at first glance, but its surface sheen offers a gentle nuance. For the city businesswoman who combines gentleness with toughness.

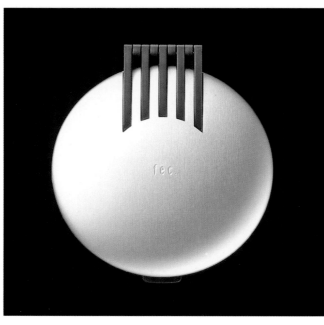

Acaciane

CLIENT: Yves Rocher, Issy-Les-Moulineaux, France

DESCRIPTION OF PRODUCT: Facial care range: 1 milk and 1 lotion for day skin 200ml; 1 milk and 1 lotion for greasy skin 200ml; 1 pot and 1 lotion for regenerative skin care 40ml; 1 pot and 1 lotion for the night 40ml

DESIGNER: Dragon Rouge, Suresnes, France

DATE OF COMPLETION/PRODUCT LAUNCH: 1991

TARGET MARKET: Women in the 25-plus age group

PLACE OF SALE: Franchise boutiques and mail order

CLIENT'S BRIEF: To put over the natural dimension of the Yves Rocher range. This particular range aims to emphasize the simplicity and excellence of the product, and its pure, vegetable base.

Self conscious

CLIENT: KOSÉ Corporation, Tokyo, Japan

DESCRIPTION OF PRODUCT: Body treatment cosmetics

DESIGNER: KOSÉ Corporation Package Designing Section, Tokyo, Japan

DATE OF COMPLETION/PRODUCT LAUNCH: May, 1991

TARGET MARKET: Women of all ages

PLACE OF SALE: Retail shops and department stores

CLIENT'S BRIEF: KOSÉ is actively involved in the beauty business with the theme centralized on "promoting comfortable beauty" with the aim of increasing its market in the total beauty industry.

DESIGN RATIONALE: Form follows function. To reflect the firming and toning effect that the product has on the body, a natural human shape is used, with an accented cap top to balance this natural design. The use of blue appropriately evokes images of freshness, blue sky, and crystal clear water.

Antartic

CLIENT: Yves Rocher, Issy-les-Moulineaux, France

DESCRIPTION OF PRODUCT: Perfume

DESIGNER: Ateliers Dinand, Levallois-Perret, France

DESIGN RATIONALE: The aim was to create a bottle which would evoke images of the north, the wide open Arctic spaces appealing to men attracted by the idea of adventure. The design had to be pure, simple and rigorous. The choice of blue was obvious.

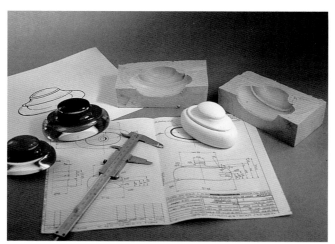

Obsession

CLIENT: Calvin Klein Cosmetics, New York, USA

DESCRIPTION OF PRODUCT: In the presentation of
Obsession, Klein has translated the amber-based scent
into the colour of the perfume bottle's mock tortoiseshell
shoulder and stopper – both modelled after the
designer's collection of rare blond tortoiseshell objects.
The bottle is a voluptuous lead crystal oval, a replica of
the mystical Indian prayer stones collected by Klein

DESIGNER: Ateliers Dinand, Levallois-Perret, France

DATE OF COMPLETION/PRODUCT LAUNCH: 1984

TARGET MARKET: Selective markets

PLACE OF SALE: Selective perfumeries

CLIENT'S BRIEF: To evoke sensuality and use of materials
(amber) loved by the fashion designer.

S de Savane

CLIENT: Smithkline Beecham, Malakoff, France

DESIGNER: Jean-Reme Guegan, Agence Ekonos, Paris, France

DATE OF COMPLETION/PRODUCT LAUNCH: November 1990

TARGET MARKET: Young, active urban men who buy their beauty cosmetics in supermarkets

DESIGN RATIONALE: To express the world of urbanity and technology by combining two materials, rubber and chrome, to make an audacious and beguiling range of products.

Henara

CLIENT: Beauty International, European Brands Group, Wallingford, Oxon, UK

DESCRIPTION OF PRODUCT: Shampoo and conditioner bottles – clear stretch-blow PET; with opticite labels and green closure. Overall height: 160mm; width: 83mm

DESIGNER: Nucleus Design Ltd, Thames Ditton, Surrey, UK

DATE OF COMPLETION/PRODUCT LAUNCH: March 1990

TARGET MARKET: B, C1, C2 women interested in hair-conditioning products, and sympathetic to use of natural products

PLACE OF SALE: Supermarkets, chemist chains and independents

CLIENT'S BRIEF: The brief was to create a new presentation for the Henara range of beauty shampoos and conditioners that would build the brand from being a specialist product range to the size and status of a mainstream haircare brand.

DESIGN RATIONALE: To develop an impactful brand presentation which accurately reflects the true brand values of naturalness and feminity, while adding a timeless quality to appeal to the market of the 1990s. Nucleus developed a strong cohesive presentation by combining unique physical packaging, surface graphics and reformulating product colours, texture and fragrance.

Cap Soleil

CLIENT: Yves Rocher, Issy Les Moulineaux, France

DESCRIPTION OF PRODUCT: Sun lotion

DESIGNER: Rodanthi Senduka/Lewis Moberly, London, UK

PHOTOGRAPHER: David Gill

DATE OF COMPLETION/PRODUCT LAUNCH: 1990

TARGET MARKET: Mothers, for family care

PLACE OF SALE: Yves Rocher, throughout France (specialist toiletries shops)

Tentatrice

CLIENT: Shiseido Co Ltd, Tokyo, Japan

PRODUCT: Tentatrice

DESCRIPTION OF PRODUCT: Perfume

DESIGNER: Tetsuo Togasawa, Tokyo, Japan

DATE OF COMPLETION/PRODUCT LAUNCH: 1990

PLACE OF SALE: Shiseido chain stores

DESIGN RATIONALE: The oriental orchid fragrance is unique. It conveys the image of the pure, gentle, oriental orchid.

Sapporo Beer

CLIENT: Sapporo Ltd, Tokyo, Japan

DESCRIPTION OF PRODUCT: Aluminium can

DESIGNER: Sapporo Ltd Design Department

DATE OF COMPLETION/PRODUCT LAUNCH: 1987

PLACE OF SALE: Off-licences, pubs and supermarkets, in UK and USA

DESIGN RATIONALE: Created to appeal to youth market, particularly for export

Matisse Yoghurt

CLIENT: United Distillers/Verbunt, Tilburg, Netherlands

DESCRIPTION OF PRODUCT: A 15 per cent liqueur on the basis of melon and yoghurt

DESIGNER: Rob van den Berg, Millford-Van den Berg Design, Wassenaar, Netherlands

ILLUSTRATOR: Hans Reisinger

DATE OF COMPLETION: 1986

TARGET MARKET: Women between 20—40 years old, outgoing and interested in exotic flavours

PLACE OF SALE: Off-licences

CLIENT'S BRIEF: To develop a design that instantly communicates the unique combination of yoghurt, melon and alcohol. This design has to break through the clutter on the shelves in off-licences. The design has to be attractive to young and modern women interested in exotic flavours.

DESIGN RATIONALE: The combination of the natural colours of melon and yoghurt will lead to an almost cosmetic signal that appeals only to women. The name Matisse indicates softness and delicateness. The unusual and intriguing design will create a unique identity which will stand out from the other liqueurs. The design breaks the codes of the liqueurs market but being sold in off-licences it will certainly communicate the main message of the briefing – instant communication of the combination of yoghurt, melon and alcohol.

Antipasto

CLIENT: J Sainsbury PLC, London, UK

DESCRIPTION OF PRODUCT: A range of Antipasto for use in cooking or as hors d'oeuvres

DESIGNER: Bottle design: Eugenio Beltrami, graphics Worhington & Co, London, UK

DATE OF COMPLETION/PRODUCT LAUNCH: Autumn 1991

TARGET MARKET: ABC1 women interested in cooking – particularly Italian food

PLACE OF SALE: Sainsbury's multiple stores

CLIENT'S BRIEF: To produce a range of quality ethnic products to appeal to adventurous men and women interested in extending their food experience.

DESIGN RATIONALE: To reflect the above in the design concept.

8ᵉ Jour

CLIENT: Yves Rocher, Issy-Les-Moulineaux, France

DESCRIPTION OF PRODUCT: Eau de toilette 100ml; eau
de toilette 50ml; eau de parfum 30ml

DESIGNER: Ateliers Dinand, Levallois-Perret, France

DATE OF COMPLETION/PRODUCT LAUNCH: 1991

TARGET MARKET: Mass market (women)

PLACE OF SALE: Yves Rocher boutiques and mail order

CLIENT'S BRIEF: To create a perfume bottle for a new
woman, that is timeless, with the colours of earth and light.

Volupté d'Oscar de la Renta

CLIENT: Sanofi Beauté Inc, New York, USA

DESCRIPTION OF PRODUCT: Avant-garde bottle with assymetric form. The "O" form stopper takes its inspiration from the design

DESIGNER: Ateliers Dinand, Levallois-Perret, France

DATE OF COMPLETION/PRODUCT LAUNCH: 1992

TARGET MARKET: Women of the 1990s

PLACE OF SALE: Selective perfumeries

CLIENT'S BRIEF: To create a brand image that would appeal to the modern, sophisticated woman

DESIGN RAATIONALE: To capture in three-dimensional form the sophistication, elegance and confidence that characterize the women of the '90s.

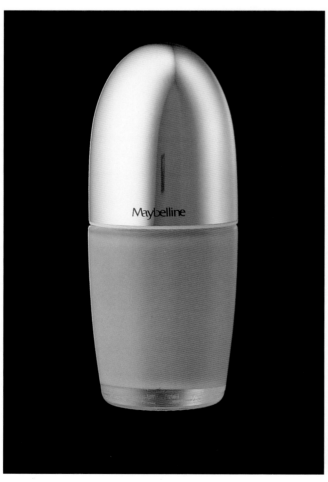

Maybelline Make-Up Series

CLIENT: Maybelline Co Ltd, Tokyo, Japan

DESCRIPTION OF PRODUCT: Materials are resin, glass and aluminium. Sizes are: single eye colour: top and bottom 37.5mm × right and left 47mm × depth 10mm; active look face colour: top and bottom 82mm × right and left 62mm × depth 15mm; active look lip stick: top and bottom 72mm × diameter 20mm; perfect nail colour: top and bottom 72mm × diameter 30mm.

DESIGNER: Taku Satoh, Tokyo, Japan

DATE OF PRODUCT LAUNCH: September 1990

TARGET MARKET: 20-year-old women who are sensitive to trends

PLACE OF SALE: Throughout Japan

CLIENT'S BRIEF: To be appropriate for young women in cities who have acquired a new sense of values, and can easily purchase and enjoy their make-up.

Café "PRÉMIO"

CLIENT: Mitsubishi Corporation, Tokyo, Japan

DESCRIPTION OF PRODUCT: Aluminium can; size: 44mm × 172.7mm

DESIGNER: GK Graphics Incorporated, Tokyo, Japan

DATE OF COMPLETION/PRODUCT LAUNCH: December 1988

TARGET MARKET: National brand for department store

PLACE OF SALE: Japan

DESIGN RATIONALE: To introduce in a gourmet gift market the concept of an aluminium canister, the first time for its kind. It was designed to express a futuristic image.

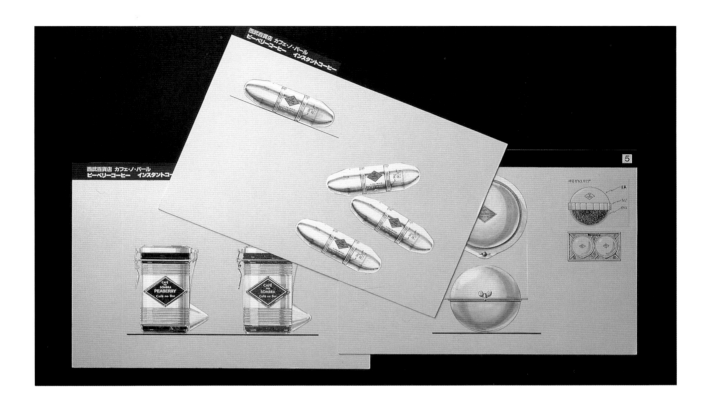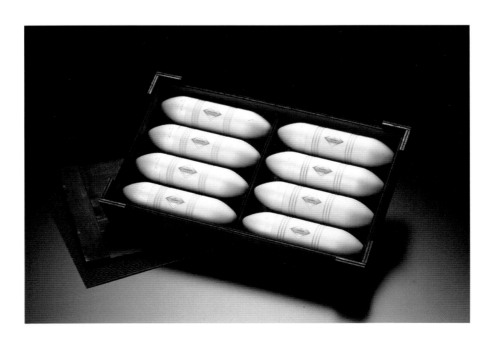

Functional   When a designer and a marketing manager sit down to discuss a packaging brief, one aspect of it will usually be added value. "How can we steal a lead on the competition? What can we provide that will give an increased incentive to the customer to buy our product rather than that of the competition? If it is a liquid shower soap, we could put a hook so that it can hang from the shower; if it's glue, we could give it a self-sealing spout that doubles as a spreading spatula."

The lines of responsibility become very blurred between the product designer and the packaging specialist in the search for this extra dimension, with products that include spouts, handles, measuring caps, and dispensing mechanisms. Clever ideas, like combining two strengths of suntan oil in one bottle, or water in a bottle (for joggers) with a spout that you open and reseal with your mouth seem to totally transform their contents, as well as keeping the products in tune with their customers' changing lifestyles.

Free and Free

CLIENT: Lion, Tokyo, Japan

DESCRIPTION OF PRODUCT: Haircare range

DESIGNER: Vitrac Strategy, Paris, France

TARGET MARKET: People, mainly women, who care
about their hair

PLACE OF SALE: Haircare salons

Vitalité

CLIENT: Coparel Vademecum, Nanterre, France

PRODUCT: Shower/shampoo Mont St Michel 'Vitalité'

DESCRIPTION OF PRODUCT: Polypropylene container than can be stood on its head or suspended

DESIGNER: Vitrac Design Strategy, Paris, France

DATE OF PRODUCT LAUNCH: April 1989

TARGET MARKET: Young clientèle

PLACE OF SALE: Department stores etc

CLIENT'S BRIEF: To bring a new aesthetic and practical design to a product.

DESIGN RATIONALE: The decoration matches the content of the product and the practical construction (the engraved ridges prevent slip) was a new departure.

House Days (Series)

CLIENT: House Food Industrial Co Ltd, Tokyo, Japan

DESCRIPTION OF PRODUCT: The materials are glass and resin. The label is paper. Size: Top and bottom: 125mm × right and left 52mm × depth 36mm. Top and bottom: 85mm × right and left 50mm × depth 36mm

DESIGNER: Taku Satoh, Tokyo, Japan

DATE OF PRODUCT LAUNCH: September 1990

TARGET MARKET: People who care about the environment

PLACE OF SALE: Throughout Japan

CLIENT'S BRIEF: The design had to be a fashionable spice bottle so that people who care about their living environment could use it.

DESIGN RATIONALE: Spice bottles designed to be pu on the table are based on the idea that they are part of the interior design. A one-touch new cap has been adopted.

UHU Flinke Flasche

CLIENT: UHU Vertriebs GmbH, Baden, Netherlands

DESCRIPTION OF PRODUCT: Glue bottle for hold-all liquid glue. The special cap is adjustable by turning to apply glue in spots or spaciously. The bottle is blow-moulded from polyethylene, the cap is injection-moulded from polyethylene too. The packaging is available in the following sizes: 35g and 90g.

DESIGNER: Studio Halm, Herne, Netherlands

DATE OF PRODUCT LAUNCH: 1980

TARGET MARKET: Kindergartens, schools, households and craftworkers

PLACE OF SALE: Stationers and art and craft shops

CLIENT'S BRIEF: The client found out that a competitive product with a spreading mechanism was very successful in the market. The task for the designer was to develop a simple spreading mechanism with better handling.

DESIGN RATIONALE: Most glues were sold in tubes which children found hard to handle. The purpose of the design was to make the secure handling of the glue bottle and the spreading mechanism suitable for children.

Pritt Bastelkleber

CLIENT: Henkel KGaA, Düsseldorf, Germany

DESCRIPTION OF PRODUCT: The packaging is a glue bottle for craftwork and contact glue. The glue bottle is equipped with a special cap with integrated folding spatula to spread the glue if necessary. The packaging is available in the following sizes: 30g and 100g.

DESIGNER: Studio Halm, Herne

DATE OF PRODUCT LAUNCH: 1989

TARGET MARKET: Kindergartens, schools, households, craftworkers

PLACE OF SALE: Stationers and art and craft shops.

CLIENT'S BRIEF: The task was to find a simple way to apply glue in spots or spread wide. The toothed spatula also was considered necessary to obtain the best adhesion of the pasted parts.

DESIGN RATIONALE: The aim was to combine diverse functions in one glue bottle: a sealable dispenser; a storage hook, a folding spatula, and a cover for the latter.

Escape by Calvin Klein

CLIENT: Calvin Klein Cosmetics, New York, USA

DESCRIPTION OF PRODUCT: A fragrance for women who like to travel. The bottle itself is glass with a silver top, and a special double closure

DESIGNER: Pierre Dinand, Ateliers Dinand, Levallois-Perret, France

DATE OF COMPLETION/PRODUCT LAUNCH: 1991

TARGET MARKET: Selective

PLACE OF SALE: High-class perfumery shops and stores

CLIENT'S BRIEF: To create a new perfume bottle in an existing range. The bottle to be based on an antique perfume bottle in Calvin Klein's wife's collection.

DESIGN RATIONALE: To create a bottle that was easy to carry around, but still looked elegant and feminine.

Arrogantissima

DESCRIPTION OF PRODUCT: Perfume, eau de parfum and
eau de toilette
DESIGNER: Ateliers Dinand, Levallois-Perret, France
DATE OF COMPLETION/PRODUCT LAUNCH: 1985
PLACE OF SALE: Pharmacies, department stores,
perfumeries etc.

Beauté Douce

CLIENT: Shu Uemura, Tokyo, Japan

DESCRIPTION OF PRODUCT: Make-up remover in a container that is both supple and solid, with a dispenser

DESIGNER: Vitrac Design Strategy, Paris, France

DATE OF PRODUCT LAUNCH: 1991

TARGET MARKET: Women in the 30 to 50 age range

PLACE OF SALE: Shu Uemura pharmacies

CLIENT'S BRIEF: To bring a new look to a product launched originally in 1967 and recently revised.

DESIGN RATIONALE: A new type of container was needed to give the product an up-to-date look.

El Charro

CLIENT: Euroitalia, Monza, Italy

DESCRIPTION OF PRODUCT: The body of the flask is in polished glass with a silver stopper. On the top of the stopper a turquoise is incorporated, reminiscent of those used by Mexican craftsmen in their traditional necklaces. A small silver chain completes the design.

DESIGNER: Ateliers Dinand, Levallois-Perret, France

DATE OF COMPLETION/PRODUCT LAUNCH: 1992

TARGET MARKET: Young, lively women who like nature and open spaces

PLACE OF SALE: El Charro boutiques and selective perfumeries

CLIENT'S BRIEF: To create a perfume bottle design that would appeal to the target market and also symbolize the idea behind the El Charro fashion label.

Night & Day: Griesser

CLIENT: Coiffure et Beauté, Geneva, Switzerland

DESCRIPTION OF PRODUCT: A 50ml glass pot and black plastic cap (70 × 45 × 40mm)

DESIGNER: Thierry Lecoule Design, Paris, France

ILLUSTRATOR/PHOTOGRAPHER: Christophe Tournebize

DATE OF COMPLETION/PRODUCT LAUNCH: End of 1987

TARGET MARKET: The Night & Day cosmetic line is aimed at middle-aged women

PLACE OF SALE: Hair Beauty Institutes in Geneva and Gstaat

CLIENT'S BRIEF: To create the right skincare product for an international élite, the top executive women who are Claus Griesser's customers.

DESIGN RATIONALE: The main aim for this creation was to have a good-looking and very specific product that broke with the tradition of skincare products. Its architectural inspiration and originality match with the high standard of the cosmetic formulation and Clauss Griesser's personality.

Soltan

CLIENT: The Boots Company plc, Nottingham, UK

DESCRIPTION OF PRODUCT: Sun-care range of toiletries

DESIGNER: Jimmy Yang/Lewis Moberly, London, UK

PHOTOGRAPHER: David Gill

DATE OF COMPLETION/PRODUCT LAUNCH: April 1991

TARGET MARKET: Mothers – for family care

PLACE OF SALE: Boots the Chemists, throughout the UK

CLIENT'S BRIEF: To design packaging that gave Soltan a modern, more relevant image and, in parallel, to make the structure more practical and pleasing. Consumers today are more concerned with protection than with baking in the sun. The shadow palm tree underscores this element.

DESIGN RATIONALE: The new structures slip easily into a bag or pocket and provide robust, leak-proof containers which dispense easily and do not gather sand at the beach. The graphics evoke happy holiday memories and, through the shadow device, suggest the important element of protection.

Direct

CLIENT: Cussons UK Ltd, Manchester, UK

DESCRIPTION OF PRODUCT: Auto dishwash liquid/powder

DESIGNER: Klaus Wuttke & Partners, London, UK

DATE OF COMPLETION/PRODUCT LAUNCH: 1991

TARGET MARKET: Dishwasher users

PLACE OF SALE: Supermarkets

CLIENT'S BRIEF: To create a striking pack for dishwasher liquids

DESIGN RATIONALE: To create a successful brand of dishwasher products

J Sainsbury's
Dishwasher Products

CLIENT: J Sainsbury PLC, London, UK

DESCRIPTION OF PRODUCT: Dishwasher powder and granular salt. The bottles are the manufacturer's stock components

DESIGNER: Via Design, London, UK

ILLUSTRATOR: In-house illustration by Sarah Laver

DATE OF PRODUCT LAUNCH: 1991

TARGET MARKET: Anyone shopping at Sainsbury's stores

PLACE OF SALE: All UK Sainsbury & Savacentre stores

CLIENT'S BRIEF: To re-design new and existing products within the range to offer an effective and economical alternative to the brand leaders "Finish" and "Sun", without compromising Sainsbury's range.

DESIGN RATIONALE: The considered use of type and colour, on stark backgrounds, conveys the effective cleaning power of these products. Original illustrations suggest the watery environment in which the products are used, all resulting in a contemporary design which is obviously "own label".

Washing Powder/Liquid

CLIENT: J Sainsbury Plc, London, UK

DESCRIPTION OF PRODUCT: Range of washing liquids and powders. The concentrated washing liquid has special measuring cap

DESIGNER: Coley Porter Bell, London, UK

DATE OF COMPLETION/PRODUCT LAUNCH: 1990

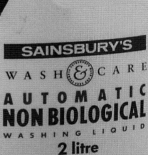

"Les Sensations"

CLIENT: Total/Cofidep, Paris (La Défense), France

DESCRIPTION OF PRODUCT: Transparent paint container
for the brand "AVI".

DESIGNER: Packaging Innovation Ltd, London, UK

DATE OF COMPLETION/PRODUCT LAUNCH: January 1991

TARGET MARKET: "Avantgarde" home decorators

PLACE OF SALE: DIY superstores in France

CLIENT'S BRIEF: The task was to create an image
evocative of the name "Les Sensations", with immediate
aesthetic appeal.

DESIGN RATIONALE: The pack is transparent with a
printed shrink sleeve. Each of the range of 14 colours is
clearly visible through a window which shows a house
interior in perspective through which the paint colour is
revealed. The pack incorporates many practical features
which make it easy to use. These include an integrated
sliding handle, a lid which can be opened and closed
without the use of an implement, and an effective
pouring lip.

Novemail Plus

CLIENT: IPA Novemail, Paris, France

DESCRIPTION OF PRODUCT: Matt, satin and gloss finish paint, without smell or toxic chemicals, which can be diluted with water

DESIGNER: Dragon Rouge, Suresnes, France

DATE OF COMPLETION/PRODUCT LAUNCH: March 1989

TARGET MARKET: Decoration and DIY enthusiasts

PLACE OF SALE: All DIY stores

CLIENT'S BRIEF: The product is innovative: The design needed to put this over – particularly the good quality, the ease of use and the originality of the product.

DESIGN RATIONALE: A new type of top made opening and closing easy, and it also allowed the customer to see the contents of the pots.

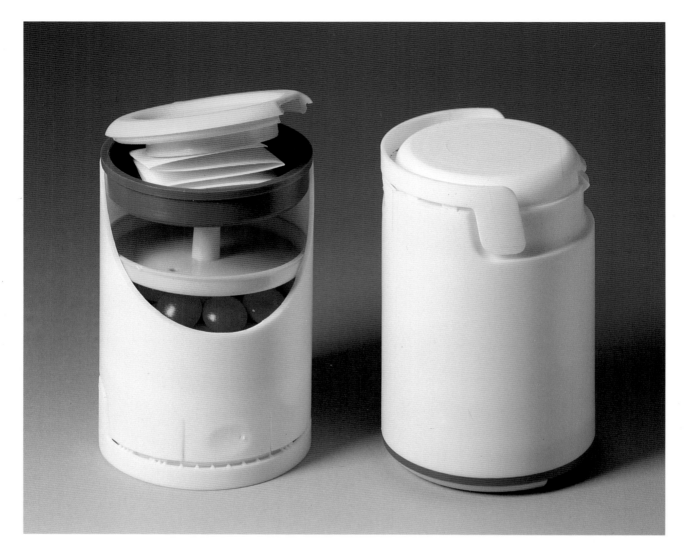

Duma

CLIENT: Duma International, Stockholm, Sweden

PRODUCT: Duma-SP System

DESCRIPTION: Polypropylene child-resistant, tamper-evident container with unique design features for solid-dose medicines.

DESIGNER: Bernard Sams, Sams Design, London, UK

CONSULTANT: Cyril Poore, New Malden Street, Surrey, UK

ILLUSTRATOR/PHOTOGRAPHER: Glyn Mead

DATE OF COMPLETION/PRODUCT LAUNCH: Early 1992

TARGET MARKET: World-wide pharmaceutical market for solid-dose medicines where maximum security, patient information and compliance are required.

PLACE OF SALE: Dispensaries everywhere

CLIENT'S BRIEF: Duma International commissioned the designer and consultant to meet the following: the reassurance of total product security; the facility to include patient information leaflets without outer cartons; variable fill capacity to meet requirements of OPD = (Original Pack Dispensing); instant evidence of tampering; child resistance, but ease of conversion for use by the elderly or arthritic; environmentally-acceptable polypropylene manufacturing components.

DESIGN RATIONALE: Duma SP was designed to meet more than ever before the needs of doctors, pharmacists and patients. At the same time it needed to appeal to production as well as marketing management by offering cost-effective integration with the manufacturing process, maximum filling flexibility and efficiency of inventory control.

C4 Tissues

CLIENT: Unitech, Tokyo, Japan

DESCRIPTION OF PRODUCT: Wet tissues for the car

DESIGNER: Yosei Kawaji Design Office, Tokyo, Japan

DATE OF COMPLETION/PRODUCT LAUNCH: September, 1990

CLIENT'S BRIEF: One of a range of car accessories in C4's brand. As a car accessory the tissues are designed to be user-friendly to use, with a convenient hook.

DESIGN RATIONALE: (Awarded a special prize in 1991 Japan Package Design Yearbook)

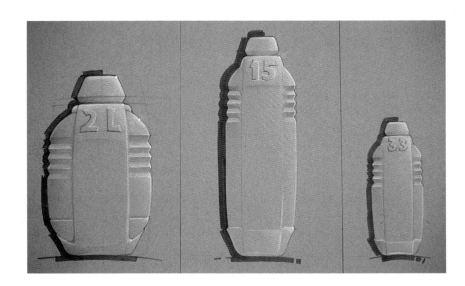

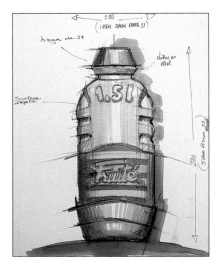

Fruité

CLIENT: Société des Eaux Minérales d'Evian, Levallois-Perret, France

DESCRIPTION OF PRODUCT: A 2 litre bottle of soft drink for children. The material is in PET

DESIGNER: Lonsdale Design, Boulogne, France

DATE OF COMPLETION/PRODUCT LAUNCH: 1989

TARGET MARKET: Children between 6 and 10 years old

PLACE OF SALE: Big stores and supermarkets

CLIENT'S BRIEF: In order to compete for leadership with other brands or similar products, Evian decided to create a specific shape for its beverage "Fruité". The main purpose is to entice children aged from 6 to 10 years old to buy the product.

DESIGN RATIONALE: Lonsdale has created the "Robot": a new shape, which is entertaining for the children, and also acceptable to their mothers.

Glacier Water Bottle

CLIENT: Glacier Water Co, Whitestone, New York, USA

DESCRIPTION OF PRODUCT: The bottle is plastic. The size is H: 17cm, W: 7cm, packaged as a disposable sports bottle.

DESIGNER: Philippe Starck, Paris, France

PHOTOGRAPHER: Kulbir Thandi

DATE OF COMPLETION/PRODUCT LAUNCH: 1991

TARGET MARKET: Young sporting people

CLIENT'S BRIEF: To create a pure, simple and refreshing design, like the drink it represents.

DESIGN RATIONALE: The watergrade plastic bottle eliminates taste and odour associated with traditional packages. It has a push-pull spout that can be opened with the teeth. The design is simple, but the concept is revolutionary.

IADA

CLIENT: IADA, Sant Just Desvern, Spain

DESCRIPTION OF PRODUCT: Plastic oil-can for cars;
size: 18.5 × 24.5 × 8cm.

DESIGNER: André Ricard, Barcelona, Spain

ILLUSTRATOR: Enric Rion

DATE OF COMPLETION/PRODUCT LAUNCH: 1989

TARGET MARKET: Motorists

PLACE OF SALE: Petrol stations

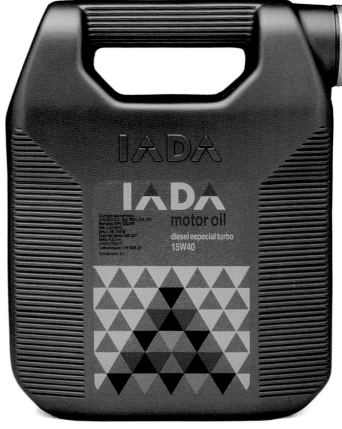

Jetmax

CLIENT: Conoco Limited, London, UK

DESCRIPTION OF PRODUCT: 5 and 1 litre packs for lubricating oil with anti-glug pouring

DESIGNER: Packaging Innovation Limited, London, UK

DATE OF COMPLETION/PRODUCT LAUNCH: May 1991

TARGET MARKET: UK motorists

PLACE OF SALE: Conoco garage forecourts

CLIENT'S BRIEF: To raise the quality perception of the brand while retaining its value-for-money image through the structure of the pack.

DESIGN RATIONALE: The pack shape is definitive in terms of branding, having been specifically designed to be completely different from more traditional oil containers which tend to be overtly technical. The Jet motor oil container has a softer, more domestic, look, more on the lines of a vacuum flask than the usual "engineered" appearance. It is very simple and "user friendly" with many special features including an integral twist top, that cannot be mislaid.

141

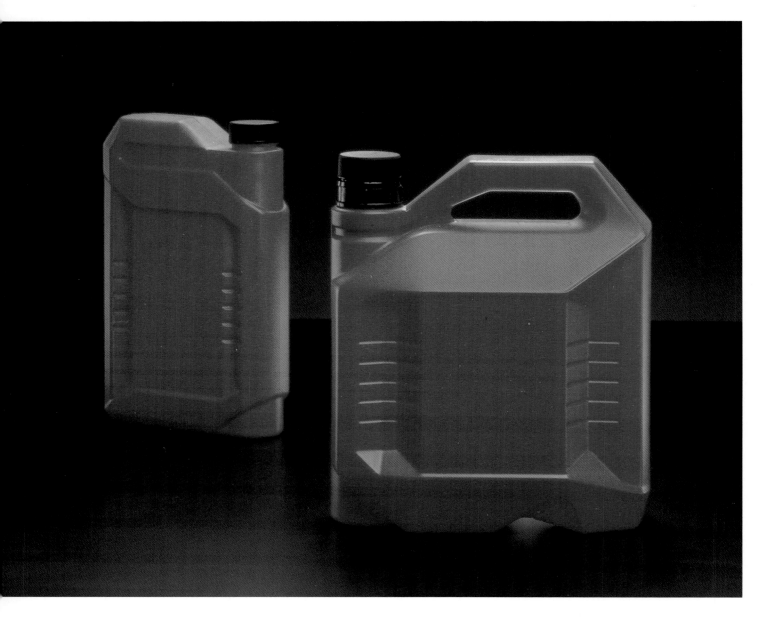

BP 2000 Lubricant Range

CLIENT: BP Oil International Ltd, London, UK

DESIGNER: Minale, Tattersfield & Partners Ltd, Richmond, Surrey, UK

TARGET MARKET: All motorists

PLACE OF SALE: BP petrol stations worldwide

CLIENT'S BRIEF: A complete reappraisal of the image and performance of the BP petrol station forecourt oil can, away from the ugly, uncomfortable; messy and sometimes dangerous tinplate ones. The new cans were also to be distributed worldwide so they comply structurally as well as appeal visually.

DESIGN RATIONALE: Minale Tattersfield created a design solution for the BP 2000 range of lubricants that was universal. There were five members of the range: black = diesel; yellow = economy; metallic dark moss green = mid-range; metallic crystal green = premium grade and metallic mid-green for the ancillary products. For the 5-and 3-litre packs a specially designed "easy flow system" – a technical ingenuity, which comprises an anti-glug restrictor in neck of the pack – was created. Ease of handling was achieved by giving packs a low centre of gravity. Specially moulded indentations created a stable handling position for pouring. The material – high-impact polyethylene – is also extremely good for recycling.

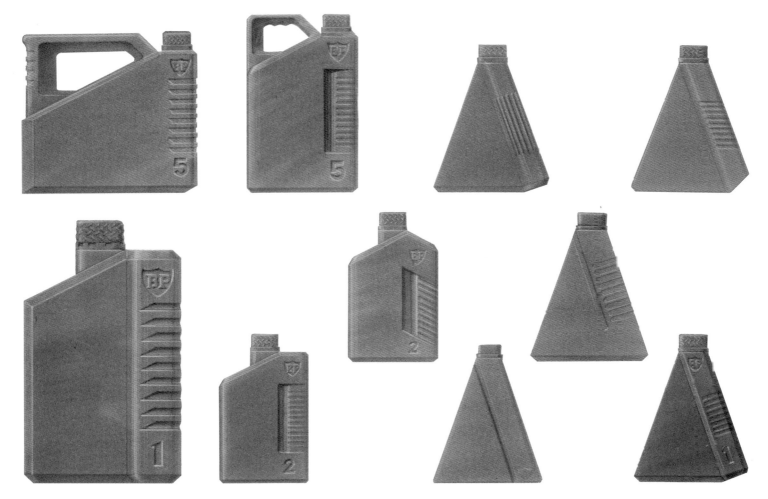

RIGHT: The dark green mid-range BP 2000 oil can, chosen for the range, and the prototypes (**BELOW**) for the final design choice.

BELOW: The BP Visco Multigrade motor oil can in sizes ranging from 500 ml to 5 litres.

Beastro

CLIENT: Bull Rodger Ltd, London, UK

DESCRIPTION OF PRODUCT: A complete
"dinner-for-one" for dogs. It is a disposable,
vacuum-formed dog's bowl with two compartments;
one with meaty chunks, the other with crunchy biscuits.
It is sealed with a tear-off foil top. Approximate size is
250mm long × 130mm wide × 50mm high

DESIGNER: Bull Rodger Ltd, London, UK

ILLUSTRATOR: Hand lettering: John Bull

DATE OF PRODUCT LAUNCH: April 1988

TARGET MARKET: Marketing personnel

PLACE OF SALE: Promoted via press advertising and
direct mail

CLIENT'S BRIEF: To develop a new product, of any kind,
to demonstrate Bull Rodger's skills in packaging design,
with a view to gaining new business in these areas.

DESIGN RATIONALE: In a world where product
development and pack design is a very serious business,
we felt there was, and still is, room for wit and
innovation, even in a crowded market like pet food. The
solution was designed to say a lot about the way we
approach our work.

Nittoh Super Tea Bag

CLIENT: Mitsui Norin Co Ltd, Tokyo, Japan

DESCRIPTION OF PRODUCT: The materials are resin and paper

DESIGNER: Taku Satoh, Tokyo, Japan

DATE OF PRODUCT LAUNCH: November 1989

TARGET MARKET: General households

PLACE OF SALE: Throughout Japan

CLIENT'S BRIEF: A new and moisture-free container was needed. It was also important to revise the image of Nittoh Tea, which had been perceived as rather low grade.

DESIGN RATIONALE: The design emphasis was on co-ordination – one pack would not stand out by itself, but would do so when displayed on shop shelves with others. In addition, in the home, the design is simple enough to match any interior.

Gift Set for No 7 Cosmetics

CLIENT: The Boots Company Ltd, Nottingham, UK

DESCRIPTION OF PRODUCT: Own brand cosmetic range for The Boots Company, packed as a gift set

DESIGNER: Salvatore Cicero, Worthington & Co, London, UK

DATE OF PRODUCT LAUNCH: 1991

TARGET MARKET: The No 7 Christmas customer is aged 18–60 and from all social categories

PLACE OF SALE: Boots Department stores in UK

DESIGN RATIONALE: The No 7 gift range had to project a sophisticated, quality and up-market positioning. The design had to appeal to the target customer (purchaser and recipient), and had to strengthen the brand image and maintain the position in the market. It also had to be festive, warm and eye-catching.

Tesco Bubble Bath

CLIENT: Tesco Stores Ltd, Waltham Cross, Herts, UK

DESCRIPTION OF PRODUCT: 250ml plastic container of
bubble bath

DESIGNER: The London Design Partnership Ltd,
London, UK

DATE OF COMPLETION/PRODUCT LAUNCH: Summer 1988

TARGET MARKET: Mothers with small children

PLACE OF SALE: Tesco's supermarkets

CLIENT'S BRIEF: To design a 3D-container and label
graphics for a bubble bath specially formulated for
children.

DESIGN RATIONALE: The choice of the hippo was natural
given the nature of the product. This, combined with the
use of primary colours and an amusing closure, gives the
product personality.

Letters/Numbers/Misfits

CLIENT: Blue Bird Confectionery Limited, Halesowen, Birmingham, UK

DESCRIPTION OF PRODUCT: Shaped, sugar-extruded sweets

DESIGNER: Fisher Ling & Bennion Limited, Cheltenham, Gloucestershire, UK

DATE OF COMPLETION/PRODUCT LAUNCH: 1988

TARGET MARKET: Mothers and children

PLACE OF SALE: Supermarkets and confectioners

CLIENT'S BRIEF: To revitalize a declining product by packaging the sweets in a beneficial and attractive format. The product had to appeal to both mothers and children.

DESIGN RATIONALE: To add value to the product, Fisher Ling & Bennion designed the packaging to have a dual purpose, not only to house the sweets, but also to become building blocks after consumption. The design added educational as well as fun values, ensuring that the product appealed to mothers and children alike.

Toblerone

CLIENT: Suchard Ltd, Cheltenham, Glos, UK

DESCRIPTION OF PRODUCT: Toblerone bar with two Cote d'Or chocolates as free offer

DESIGNER: J. Schwarz, Cheltenham, Glos, UK

DATE OF COMPLETION: 1992

TARGET MARKET: Male and female, 20–35 years old

Teenee Beanees

CLIENT: Just Born Candy, Bethlehem, Pennsylvania, USA

DESCRIPTION OF PRODUCT: Gourmet jelly-bean dispenser. Plastic injection molded canister with a clear PVC insert which divides the container into four parts, each for a different flavour jelly bean. Plus cover for dispenser

DESIGNER: Peterson & Blyth Associates, New York, USA

TARGET MARKET: Both children and adults

PLACE OF SALE: Supermarkets and department stores

CLIENT'S BRIEF: To set this gourmet jelly bean apart from the competition and make it easy for consumers to select their favourite flavour candy.

DESIGN RATIONALE: Teenee Beanees' packaging is a technical feat from both a packaging and printing perspective. What's unusual about this job is the high level of precision achieved with the flexographic printing process used for the labels. Despite the fact that the illustrations are very intricate, not a trace of detail or any colour clarity was lost. The label for each of the seven assortments bears a fanciful vignette bordered by a still-life of the appropriate fruit. The die cut labels give the product a high-quality, almost three-dimensional look. Furthermore, the white high-gloss labels have a removable adhesive which makes it easy for consumers to use the container afterwards when the candy is finished.

Pressé

CLIENT: Colourstyle Limited, London, UK

DESCRIPTION OF PRODUCT: A range of paper pulp folders containing a choice of stationery

DESIGNER: Nigel Goode, Priestman Associates, London, UK

DATE OF COMPLETION/PRODUCT LAUNCH: February 1992

PLACE OF SALE: Retail outlets and mail order

CLIENT'S BRIEF: The product was initiated by Priestman Associates, who designed and developed the range of products which are being manufactured and marketed by Colourstyle Ltd.

DESIGN RATIONALE: The material of the main mouldings have previously only been used for low-value disposable items such as egg boxes, as it was thought to be rough and unattractive. We felt that the tactile quality and the handmade look of items manufactured in this material offer something new in the world of identical crisply shaped, smooth-finished products.

Account Opening Pack

CLIENT: Lloyds Bank plc, Bristol, UK

DESCRIPTION OF PRODUCT: A black injection-moulded polypropylene case, with a living hinge, 285 × 315 × 30mm, containing heat-sealed inner units for filing made of semi-rigid PVC with metal stud filing posts

DESIGNER: Amanda Tatham, Tatham Pearce Ltd, London, UK with Weaver Associates, London, UK

DATE OF COMPLETION/PRODUCT LAUNCH: February 1990

TARGET MARKET: Prospective Lloyds Bank account customers

PLACE OF SALE: The product is given free at Lloyds Bank branches

CLIENT'S BRIEF: To design an item of real value, within a restricted budget, to be given free to customers. As "the place to keep Lloyds Bank information at home", it files statements, contact details, marketing material, cheque books, etc. Alternatively customers can use it for their own purposes, such as a small briefcase.

DESIGN RATIONALE: To produce large numbers within a given budget and to avoid the "cheapness" of the usual free items, it was decided to make this an injection-moulded case, building flexibility into the tool for new features in future. Tactile qualities, including a simple snap-shut device, were important as was the use of smart corporate black.

Real Deodorant (Structure)

CLIENT: The Mennen Company, Morristown, New Jersey, USA

DESCRIPTION OF PRODUCT: A mushroom-shaped plastic deodorant dispenser

DESIGNER: Gerstman+Meyers Inc, New York, USA

DATE OF COMPLETION/PRODUCT LAUNCH: 1980

TARGET MARKET: Male and female users of deodorant

PLACE OF SALE: Grocery and drug stores in various markets throughout the United States

CLIENT'S BRIEF: The Mennen Company had developed a new anti-perspirant cream that looked and felt like a powder. When applied by the user, the anti-perspirant quickly disappeared. At the time, there was no other product with these specific characteristics, so Mennen wanted to create an applicator/display unit that would capitalize on this product's unique quality.

DESIGN RATIONALE: Gerstman+Meyer's deodorant dispenser design addresses the ergonomic requirements needed to ensure the proper application of the product. A new and innovative mushroom-shaped dispenser unit was created that is both convenient and attractive.

Tahiti

CLIENT: Unilever-Johnson, UK

DESCRIPTION OF PRODUCT: Tahiti shower gel

DESIGNER: Desgrippes Cato Gobe Group, Paris, France

DATE OF COMPLETION/PRODUCT LAUNCH: 1991

TARGET MARKET: Europe

PLACE OF SALE: Mass market

CLIENT'S BRIEF: Tahiti is the European leader in the shower products and bubble-bath market. The client wanted to update its brand image and to develop one sole packaging for all European countries.

DESIGN RATIONALE: The designer's response was to focus on the brand's strongest elements – the name and the famous cubic shape of its shower products – and to create a signature incorporating the square and introducing an exotic symbol, which played on a variety of colours.

Protective   The most basic form of packaging is that which is provided simply to protect the product or the contents. Fairly basic, you might think, and in Germany this form of packaging is being manufactured so that it can be removed and discarded in specially provided bins outside the stores.

Protective packs can prevent half-a-dozen eggs from breaking, but they can also prevent half-a-dozen cans of beer from getting damaged (as well as providing a useful carrying handle). But there are also more prestigious forms.

In this chapter, I have included wine shipped in a hand-crafted wooden box for clients as a Christmas gift; tawny port packed with fragile Cheddar cheese; a watch strap in a sleeve so you can try it on without unwrapping it, and a cup and saucer packed in an ingenious cardboard construction.

Morris of Rutherglen Liqueur Fortified Range

CLIENT: Morris Wines Pty Ltd, Victoria, Australia

DESCRIPTION OF PRODUCT: 750ml bottle and gift cylinder for Liqueur Muscat, Liqueur Tokay and Old Tawny Port

DESIGNER: Barrie Tucker/Jody Tucker, Barrie Tucker Design Pty Ltd, Eastwood, South Australia

ILLUSTRATOR/PHOTOGRAPHER: Jody Tucker/Dover

DATE OF COMPLETION/PRODUCT LAUNCH: January 1991

PLACE OF SALE: Bottle shops and restaurants throughout Australia

CLIENT'S BRIEF: The packaging design had to project the quality and tradition of the wine company, the Morris family and the individual products, as well as being presented in packages that were attractive for gift-giving.

DESIGN RATIONALE: To create a set of three "story books", illustrated history lessons, souvenir items, gift boxes and, by the way, wine packaging.

Yalumba Ten Year Old Premium Port

CLIENT: S. Smith & Son Pty Ltd, Angaston, Australia

DESCRIPTION OF PRODUCT: Premium port packaged in a 750ml bottle and gift cylinder

DESIGNER: Barrie Tucker/Elizabeth Schlooz, Barrie Tucker Design Pty Ltd, Eastwood, South Australia

DATE OF COMPLETION/PRODUCT LAUNCH: October 1988

PLACE OF SALE: Bottle shops and restaurants throughout Australia

CLIENT'S BRIEF: Since 1986, there have been changes in the Australian premium port market. A niche opened in the market between commercial premium ports and deluxe tawny ports. With this gap came the opportunity for S. Smith & Son to launch "Yalumba Ten Year Old Premium Port" which required packaging imagery that clearly reflected the company's heritage and commitment to quality.

DESIGN RATIONALE: Cigars and port wine go well together so the designer decided that this ten-year-old port should have some of the feeling and packaging elements of a quality cigar.

Oban

CLIENT: United Distillers, London, UK

DESCRIPTION OF PRODUCT: Malt whisky (bottle and carton)

DESIGNER: Mary Lewis, Lewis Moberly, London, UK

ILLUSTRATOR: Bill Sanderson

DATE OF COMPLETION/PRODUCT LAUNCH: November 1988

TARGET MARKET: Malt whisky connoisseurs

PLACE OF SALE: Specialist outlets, duty-free outlets, supermarkets, off licences, etc.

CLIENT'S BRIEF: To design packaging that would appeal to malt whisky "academics", as well as consumers unfamiliar with malt but keen to experience the taste.

DESIGN RATIONALE: The unique bottle shape evokes the quality and prestige of malt whisky. The long copy label gives the brand a "bookish" feel and the graphics reflect the bleak, rocky West Highland coastline with its squawking gulls and bracing winds.

Boxed Wine or Port

CLIENT: Vernon Morgan, London, UK

DESCRIPTION OF PRODUCT: Pine box with slide in lid made from pine wood. Two labels, one bearing a message from the photographer, the other used as a seal. Size 270 × 85mm

DESIGNER: Graham Barker, Towcester, Northants, UK

ILLUSTRATOR/PHOTOGRAPHER: Graham Barker

DATE OF COMPLETION/PRODUCT LAUNCH: 8th December 1991

TARGET MARKET: Photographers' clients

PLACE OF SALE: Promotion only

CLIENT'S BRIEF: As a specialist food photographer working for clients with high standards, he desired a designed package that embodied a strong sense of quality and sophistication with just a touch of intrigue and humour.

DESIGN RATIONALE: The focal point of the entire package was the message on the front label. Dark ivy green, red, gold and the use of a woodcut-style illustration were employed to suggest a sense of "Englishness" and tradition.

Kiyokawa

CLIENT: Kiyokawa Shoten, Fukushima, Japan

DESCRIPTION OF PRODUCT: The materials are glass and aluminium with a paper label. The capacity is 1.8 litres

DESIGNER: Taku Satoh, Tokyo, Japan

DATE OF COMPLETION/PRODUCT LAUNCH: September 1989

TARGET MARKET: People who like nature

PLACE OF SALE: Throughout Japan

CLIENT'S BRIEF: To emphasize that this product was from districts using rice produced by organic agricultural methods.

DESIGN RATIONALE: This is for a small brewer, so the simple taste was expressed by the total package.

Nikka Whisky from the Barrel

CLIENT: Nikka Whisky Distilling Co Ltd, Tokyo, Japan

DESCRIPTION OF PRODUCT: The materials are glass and aluminium, with a paper label. The capacity is 500ml

DESIGNER: Taku Satoh, Tokyo, Japan

DATE OF COMPLETION/PRODUCT LAUNCH: 1985

TARGET MARKET: People who like living in cities

PLACE OF SALE: Throughout Japan

CLIENT'S BRIEF: Only that the whisky in this case was strong: 51.4 per cent

DESIGN RATIONALE: To express that it is just out of the barrel as the name indicates. It has a simple finish using materials (glass, aluminium and paper) with no unnecessary design factors.

Pure Malt

CLIENT: Nikka Whisky Distilling Co Ltd, Tokyo, Japan

DESCRIPTION OF PRODUCT: The materials are glass and aluminium with a paper label. The capacity is 500ml

DESIGNER: Taku Satoh, Tokyo, Japan

DATE OF COMPLETION/PRODUCT LAUNCH: 1984

TARGET MARKET: Young people who do not drink whisky

PLACE OF SALE: Throughout Japan

CLIENT'S BRIEF: This is a special product. The design was not at the client's request; the designer made a presentation and the client decided to merchandize it.

DESIGN RATIONALE: The concept of whisky so far has been sold on an individual basis, and a new whisky bottle for a new generation was proposed.

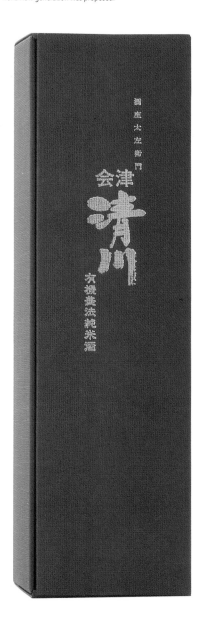

James Russell Wine Coolers

CLIENT: S Smith & Son, Angaston, South Australia

DESCRIPTION OF PRODUCT: Wine cooler (blend of wine & fruit juice) packaged in specially made 250ml bottles. Available also in 6-pack.

DESIGNER: Barrie Tucker/Elizabeth Schlooz, Barrie Tucker Design Pty Ltd, Eastwood, South Australia

DATE OF COMPLETION/PRODUCT LAUNCH: March 1987

TARGET MARKET: Specifically designed for US market only

PLACE OF SALE: Restaurants and bottle shops in USA

CLIENT'S BRIEF: To develop packaging for a more "adult" cooler for the US market. The cooler contained quality wine and pure fruit juice.

DESIGN RATIONALE: After the world explosion of wine coolers in the mid-1980s, which were targeted primarily at the young adult market and reflected this in their colourful and sometimes "wild" packaging, it became apparent that there was room in the market place for a product that, while remaining a wine/fruit juice mix, was less sweet and more "adult". The resultant image is fresh and sophisticated, and would be at home on any restaurant table.

Island Lagers

CLIENT: Sanctuary Cove Resort, Hope Island, Queensland, Australia

DESCRIPTION OF PRODUCT: Naturally brewed beer packaged in 375ml bottles and 12-bottle wooden box

DESIGNER: Barrie Tucker/Elizabeth Schooz, Barrie Tucker Design Pty Ltd, Eastwood, South Australia

DATE OF COMPLETION/PRODUCT LAUNCH: December 1987

PLACE OF SALE: Sanctuary Cove Brewery and selected bottle shops throughout Australia

CLIENT'S BRIEF: The Sanctuary Cove Brewing Company, established within Sanctuary Cove Resort, brews its own beer under the name "Island Lagers". In developing a visual identity for the company, an awareness of the broad range of applications it would fulfil was required.

DESIGN RATIONALE: For the designer, the challenge was to combine successfully a traditional brewery style with a feeling of a contemporary resort in one identity. It had to work as well on a building as on a small bottle top.

Farmers' Union Centenary Cheese and Port Packaging

CLIENT: Farmers Union Food Ltd, Mile End, South Australia

DESCRIPTION OF PRODUCT: Special rinded vintage cheddar cheese and tawny port presented in a handmade wooden box. The port came in a special ceramic bottle.

DESIGNER: Barrie Tucker/Elizabeth Schlooz, Barrie Tucker Design Pty Ltd, Eastwood, South Australia

ILLUSTRATOR: Archival Illustrators

DATE OF COMPLETION/PRODUCT LAUNCH: 1988

PLACE OF SALE: South Australia: supermarkets, speciality grocery stores, etc. Also given as a gift by the company to special clients

CLIENT'S BRIEF: To package a cheese made especially for the Farmers' Union centenary year.

DESIGN RATIONALE: To celebrate their centenary, the Farmers Union had made a special cheese but didn't know what to do with it. The designer decided that for such a special occasion, the cheese should be presented in two ways – in one with a special port wine in a quality, hand-made box and, in the other, in its own box to sell in stores.

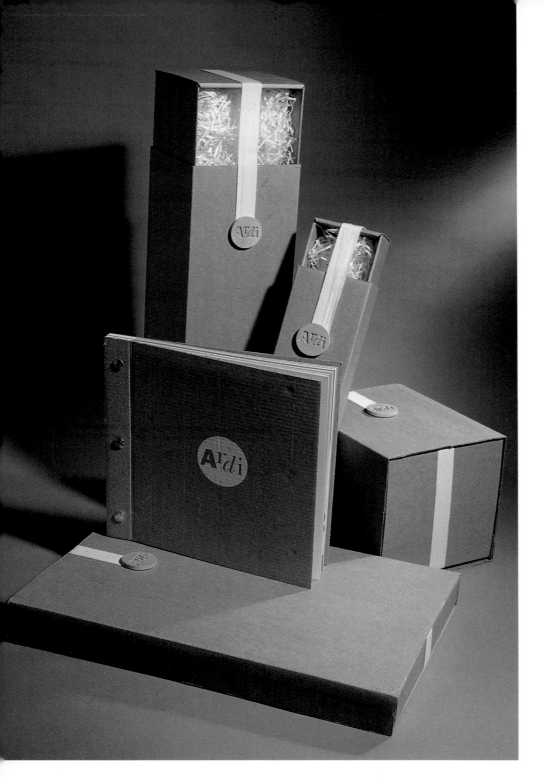

Packaging for Household Products

CLIENT: Ardi, Mere, France

DESCRIPTION OF PRODUCT: Packaging in recycled cardboard and paper for a range of household products

DESIGNER: Anne-Marie Nicol, Ardi, Mere, Montfort l'Amaury, France

PLACE OF SALE: Specialist stores for household goods, such as The Conran Shop in London, and suitable outlets in France

DESIGN RATIONALE: To create a unified image, with a strong, simple identity, in which the Ardi logo stands out.

Galilea

CLIENT: Sculptures-Jeux SA, Paris, France

DESCRIPTION OF PRODUCT: Recyclable, economic cardboard packaging printed in one colour; 24 × 12.5 × 12cm

DESIGNER: Bernard Vuarnesson, Paris, France

DATE OF PRODUCT LAUNCH: 1988

TARGET MARKET: Gift stores and catalogue sale

PLACE OF SALE: Europe, North America, Australia and Japan

BRIEF: An economic paperboard packaging was required, easily stored and folded at will, to provide good protection for transportation and also to enable it to be used as a display.

"Nou Telèfon, Nou Fax" (New telephone number, new fax number)

CLIENT: Disseny i Comunicació Ideograma, sa, Barcelona, Spain

DESCRIPTION OF PRODUCT: Total size: 280 × 115mm. Size of the printed cardboard: 100 × 210mm (offset impression). Ticket size: 105 × 57mm. It is printed with three different inking pads. The package includes 1 or 2 wood shavings. All those objects are enveloped with 1 sheet of "Cushion Wrap 3001" (280 × 350mm) of British sisalkraft

DESIGNER: Disseny i Comunicació Ideograma, SA, Barcelona, Spain

DATE OF COMPLETION/PRODUCT LAUNCH: November 1991

TARGET MARKET: Clients, suppliers and friends

CLIENT'S BRIEF: We were our own clients in this project.

DESIGN RATIONALE: We wanted to find a striking image for our mailing for clients, suppliers and friends to notify them of the change in our telephone and fax numbers. We were very careful to choose the materials that would result in a coherent approach. Our aim was to make sure people took note of the new telephone and fax of Ideograma. To that end, we enclosed a gift pencil.

Pillars of Time

CLIENT: Sculptures-Jeux S.A., Paris, France

DESCRIPTION OF PRODUCT: Recyclable, economic cardboard packaging printed in one colour; size: 17 × 11.5 × 4.5 cm

DESIGNER: Bernard Vuarnesson, Sculpture-Jeux, Paris, France

DATE OF COMPLETION/PRODUCT LAUNCH: 1992

TARGET MARKET: Gift stores and catalogue sales

PLACE OF SALE: Sold in Europe and North America

DESIGN RATIONALE: To create economic, easy-to-fold packaging, made out, as is the product itself (a perpetual calendar), of paperboard and wood, without glue, staples or any other materials.

Een moment voor jezelf
(A moment for yourself)

CLIENT: Visser Bay Anders Toscani, Amsterdam, The Netherlands

DESCRIPTION OF PRODUCT: Series of cups and saucers packed in a cardboard, pyramid form

DESIGNER: Teun Anders, Marcel Verhaaf and Martijn Leenen, Visser Bay Anders Toscani, Amsterdam, The Netherlands

ILLUSTRATORS: T. Anders, M. Leenen, T. Bakker, M. Spreeuwenberg, M. Gort, P. van Deursen, E. Bay, M. Bus, W. Kroon, M. Verhaaf, R. Verhaart and J. Wijers

DATE OF COMPLETION: March 1990

TARGET MARKET: Marketing device for potential new business

PLACE OF SALE: Promotion only

CLIENT'S BRIEF: A New Year's promotional film, reflecting the strong individual creative spirit within the company.

DESIGN RATIONALE: Each designer within the company was given a box of unglazed cups and saucers to decorate. The resulting 12 series of 40 sets were documented in an illustrated book. Each cup and saucer was packed in a pyramid shaped box with an accompanying book. In this way every recipient had an overview of the whole series.

"Le Coutances" Cheese

CLIENT: Union Laitiere Normande, France

DESCRIPTION OF PRODUCT: "Le Coutances" cheese

DESIGNER: Desgrippes Cato Gobe Group, Paris, France

DATE OF COMPLETION/PRODUCT LAUNCH: 1990

TARGET MARKET: France

PLACE OF SALE: Supermarkets and grocery stores

CLIENT'S BRIEF: L'Union Laitiere Normande wanted to create a sophisticated image, blending tradition and modernity for the mass-market product.

DESIGN RATIONALE: New packaging and decor for the cheese "Le Coutances". Created a box made of cardboard and wood. Natural materials chosen to emphasize the idea of a traditional product. The illustration of a little Normandy farm is printed within a round stamp that helps suggest the authenticity of this cheese.

Lunchbox

CLIENT: Kingcrisp, Deal, Kent, UK

DESCRIPTION OF PRODUCT: Healthy convenient packed lunch, with salad, flapjack, apple, quiche or meat

DESIGNER: Mark Baylis and Rob Howton, Jones & Co Design Ltd, London, UK

ILLUSTRATORS: Airbrush illustration: Joe Lawrence; Line drawings: Joe Santos

DATE OF COMPLETION/PRODUCT LAUNCH: Summer 1991

TARGET MARKET: Health-conscious busy professionals; school children

PLACE OF SALE: Supermarkets, service stations, small grocery stores

CLIENT'S BRIEF: The Lunchbox design had to be flexible enough to allow for different contents. A large window area and a strong on-shelf identity were also required. The wholesome qualities of the ingredients also needed to be stressed.

DESIGN RATIONALE: The wicker basket design is appropriately rustic with a fresh picnic appeal. Different varieties are then colour-coded with the use of a tamper-evident seal.

Clicker

CLIENT: Cobra, Besanson, France

DESCRIPTION OF PRODUCT: New packaging concept for
a watch bracelet

DESIGNER: Vitrac Design Strategy, Paris, France

DATE OF PRODUCT LAUNCH: 1991

TARGET MARKET: All

PLACE OF SALE: Jewellers

CLIENT'S BRIEF: To create a new system of packaging
which helps to sell the watch straps.

DESIGN RATIONALE: The packaging had to be
innovative, aesthetic and functional. The transparent
plastic packaging allows you to judge the combined
effect of watch and strap. An opening in the plastic
makes it possible for the purchaser to gauge the quality
and colour of the leather.

Liz Claiborne

CLIENT: Liz Claiborne Cosmetics, New York, USA

DESIGNER: Ateliers Dinand, Levallois-Perret, France

ILLUSTRATOR OR PHOTOGRAPHER: Patrick Rougeron

DATE OF COMPLETION/PRODUCT LAUNCH: 1986

TARGET MARKET: Selective and mass market

PLACE OF SALE: USA

Krazy Krizia

CLIENT: Profumi di Parma, Florbath, Parma, Italy

DESCRIPTION OF PRODUCT: Perfume, eau de parfum and eau de toilette in a range of sizes from 15ml to 100ml

DESIGNER: Ateliers Dinand, Levallois-Perret, France

DATE OF COMPLETION/PRODUCT LAUNCH: 1992

TARGET MARKET: Women

PLACE OF SALE: Pharmacies, department stores, perfumeries, etc.

DESIGN RATIONALE: Aimed at women with a new kind of femininity: with class, beauty and a touch of impulsivity. The bottle shape has a sensual roundness of form.

Radical

Sometimes the styling of a pack is determined by its function. The shape of a bottle is dictated by its contents or the amount of space it can take up on a shelf, or perhaps by the fact that it needs to fit into the door of a fridge. The size of the container is determined by its contents, or by shipping restrictions, or by the price point, for example.

But in this chapter I've grouped together packaging that respects none of these traditional boundaries. Here is perfume you can spin like a top; here are chocolates in miniature suitcases, and here are T-shirts in tea bags. But don't get the impression that total anarchy reigns. For example, once you get used to wine that is not in traditional wine bottles, the Georg Meisser products seem beautifully proportioned and totally desirable.

If you forget that toothpaste normally comes in tubes, the Philippe Starck Fluocaril is practical and stylish. And if you like your chocolates to be individual, the diamond-shaped Heals boxes are bold and beautiful.

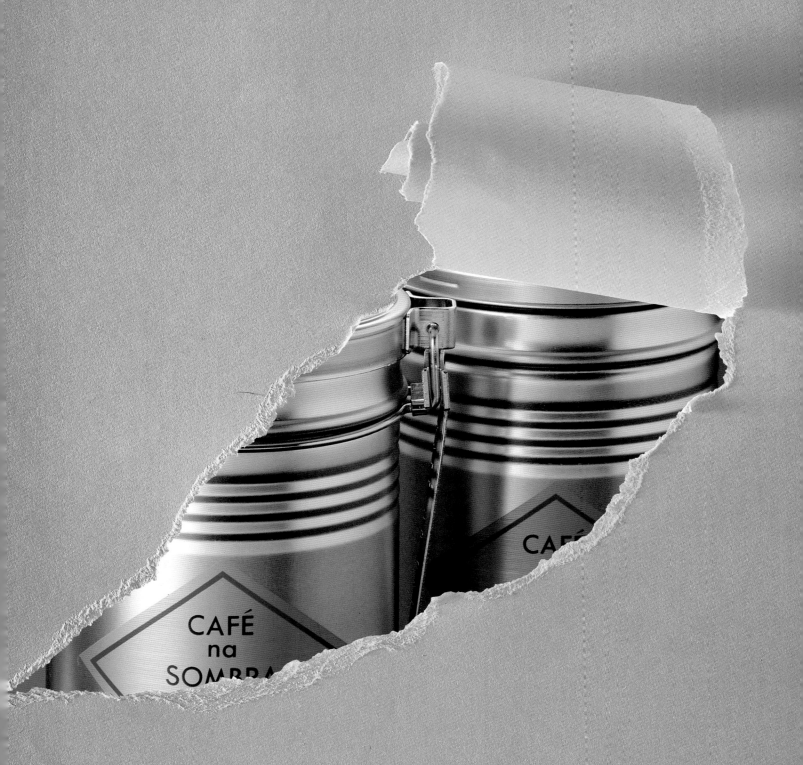

Star

DESCRIPTION OF PRODUCT: Perfume bottle in glass and
chrome

DESIGNER: Dragon Rouge, Suresnes, France

DATE OF COMPLETION/PRODUCT LAUNCH: April 1988

TARGET MARKET: Special launch on TV

DESIGN RATIONALE: The bottle was created as a
homage to Jacques Seguela, and has been part of
several travelling exhibitions.

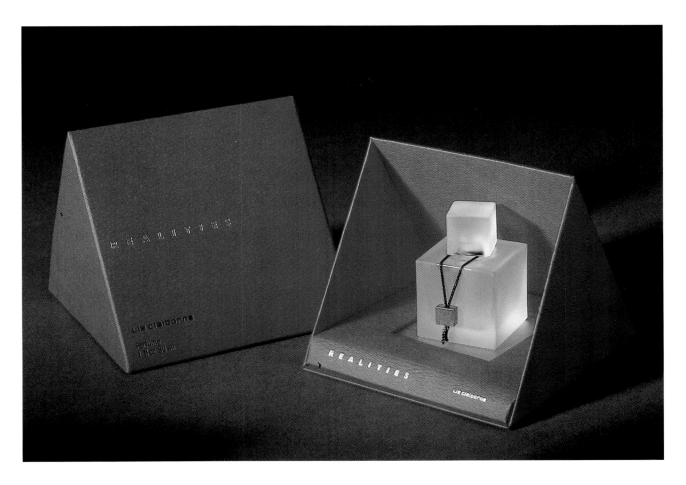

Realities

CLIENT: Liz Claiborne, Inc, New York, USA

DESCRIPTION OF PRODUCT: Women's fragrance bottles and packages for perfume, eau de cologne, and accessories

DESIGNER: Design Director: Ivan Chermayeff. Designers: Ivan Chermayeff, Lorraine Ferguson, Piera Grandesso, Chermayeff & Geismar Inc, New York, USA

DATE OF COMPLETION/PRODUCT LAUNCH: October 1990

TARGET MARKET: Women of all ages

PLACE OF SALE: Claiborne is sold in major department stores throughout the US and Canada, with potential to enter new markets in the future

CLIENT'S BRIEF: To develop a line that is sophisticated, elegant, very special and completely feminine.

DESIGN RATIONALE: Package incorporates the unexpected use of geometric shapes, and the celebration of bold and innovative colour with an elegant infusion of gold. It is noted for its geometry and broken symmetry; the classic form of the cube revolving in space; a feeling of continuity with an edge of the new; a fresh angle on a basic form packaged in a vibrant colour to set off the colours of the cubes.

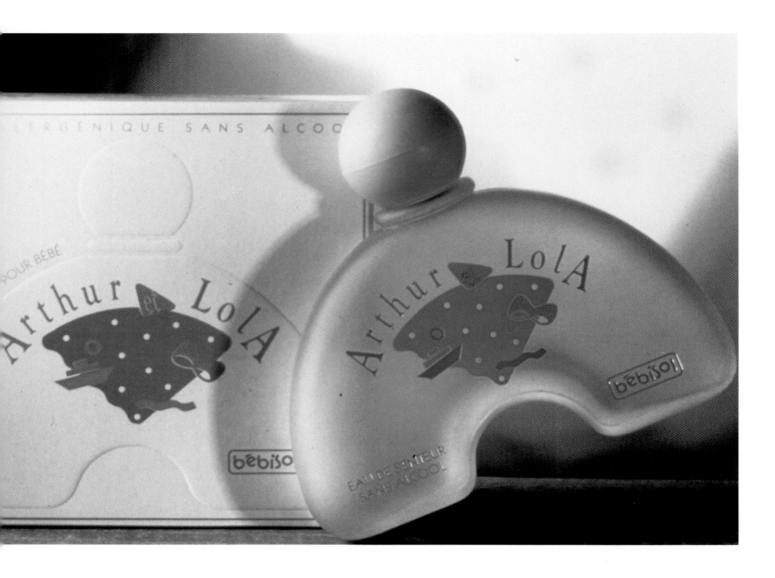

"Arthur et Lola"

CLIENT: Laboratoire Pharmygiène, Le Plessis-Robinson, France

DESCRIPTION OF PRODUCT: A baby perfume signed "Bebisol"

DESIGNER: Dominique Belle/Jean-Jacques Urvoy, Le Clan Design, Paris, France

DATE OF COMPLETION/PRODUCT LAUNCH: May 1991

TARGET MARKET: Mothers

PLACE OF SALE: Selective market pharmacies; 22,000 points of sales in France

CLIENT'S BRIEF: To create the name, the volume, the graphic design, the packaging for the baby perfume (for girls and boys). The key words of the brief were a creation between the world of pharmaceutics and cosmetics; support of the mother-baby relationship.

DESIGN RATIONALE: The plump bottle and frosted glass remind one of the pleasant sensation of a baby's skin. The product design creates a good balance between the world of pharmaceutics and the world of cosmetics, with the use of a sober white box and slightly satiny finish, and the refinement and attention to details in each phase of creation (drawing and design of volume, choice of materials, graphics and colours).

Paloma Picasso Parfum

CLIENT: Parfums Paloma Picasso, Surrey, UK

DESIGNER: River House Creative Consultants, London, UK

DATE OF COMPLETION/PRODUCT LAUNCH: September 1986

TARGET MARKET: Sophisticated women of 25 plus

PLACE OF SALE: Perfumeries and department stores

DESIGN RATIONALE: In all of Paloma Picasso's creations, her self-confidence and personal sense of style and beauty are very much in evidence. The aesthetic design of the perfume bottle echoes a jewel-like quality, revealing a golden orb of fragrance within a sculptured, frosted glass sphere.

V'e Versace

CLIENT: Versace Profumi, Lodi, Italy

DESCRIPTION OF PRODUCT: "Extrait de Parfum"
presented in a signed and numbered casket (102 × 110
× 103mm; weight 3.3kg) made from a solid block of
polished Baccarat crystal

DESIGNER: Thierry Lecoule Design, Paris, France

ILLUSTRATOR/PHOTOGRAPHER: Robert Gregoire

DATE OF COMPLETION/PRODUCT LAUNCH: End of 1989
Italy; 1990 worldwide

TARGET MARKET: All women

PLACE OF SALE: Worldwide selective perfumeries and
Gianni Versace boutiques

CLIENT'S BRIEF: To reflect Gianni Versace's couture and
to emphasize his "avant-gardisme".

DESIGN RATIONALE: From all the possible forms
requested and explored, the cube was selected as the
basis of the design. The originality of the bottle is
embodied in the power and purity of its geometric
shape. Yet at the same time, it challenges its very shape,
transforming it into an intriguing cube. Pierced by its
illusory column, the traditional cube-shape appears to
topple over, only to regain its poise in an almost magical
balance which touches the beholder.

Teatro alla Scala

CLIENT: Profumi di Parma, Florbath, Parma, Italy

DESCRIPTION OF PRODUCT: Perfume, eau de parfum and eau de toilette

DESIGNER: Ateliers Dinand, Levallois-Perret, France

DATE OF COMPLETION/PRODUCT LAUNCH: 1988

TARGET MARKET: Elegant women of 25 plus

PLACE OF SALE: Pharmacies, department stores, perfumeries, etc.

Vie Privée

CLIENT: Yves Rocher, Issy les Moulineaux, France

DESCRIPTION OF PRODUCT: Women's fragrance line

DESIGNER: Desgrippes Cato Gobe Group, Paris, France

DATE OF COMPLETION/PRODUCT LAUNCH: 1989

TARGET MARKET: France

PLACE OF SALE: Yves Rocher boutiques, selected department stores and mail order catalogues

CLIENT'S BRIEF: The natural beauty product brand, Yves Rocher, wanted to appeal to today's woman in a more contemporary way.

DESIGN RATIONALE: The inkstand-like unpolished green jade glass holds the key to a woman's secret life. The case, with its ribbon and yellow label takes its inspiration from the binding of a personal diary. The flower-shaped stopper symbolizes the fragrance.

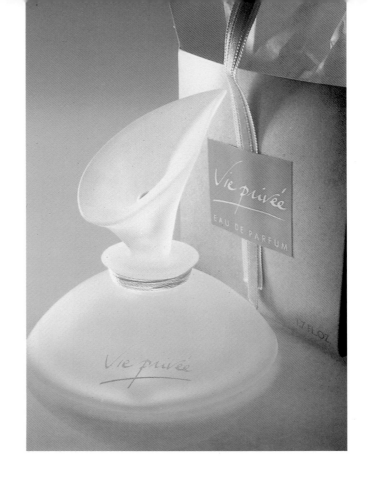

Laguna by Les Parfums Salvador Dali

CLIENT: Les Parfums Salvador Dali, Paris, France

DESCRIPTION OF PRODUCT: 100ml + 50ml eau de toilette spray together with sample phial

DESIGNER: Cofci SA, Paris, France

DATE OF COMPLETION/PRODUCT LAUNCH: May 1991 (UK launch)

TARGET MARKET: Women 15–34 years

PLACE OF SALE: Major department stores and leading perfumeries throughout the UK

DESIGN RATIONALE: Flacon design based on an original crystal flask supplied by Salvador Dali, who gained inspiration from his painting "Apparition du Visage de l'Aphrodite de Cuide" (1981).

Parfum Cartier

CLIENT: Cartier Inc, New York, USA

DESIGNER: Consumer Promotions Inc, Mount Vernon, New York, USA

DATE OF COMPLETION/PRODUCT LAUNCH: May 1989

TARGET MARKET: Female

PLACE OF SALE: Boutiques

CLIENT'S BRIEF: The objective of the design was to communicate that Parfums de Cartier is available and is a uniquely wearable art form, as is Cartier's world-famous jewellery.

Baker Street Snacks Range

CLIENT: Sisterson Foods Ltd, Consett, Durham, UK

DESCRIPTION OF PRODUCT: Free-standing block-bottomed deli-bag

DESIGNER: Blackburn's, London, UK

ILLUSTRATOR: Michael Frith

DATE OF COMPLETION/PRODUCT LAUNCH: April 1991

TARGET MARKET: ABC1; 20–45 years; adults, sophisticated and cosmopolitan in attitude

PLACE OF SALE: Major multiples and delicatessens

CLIENT'S BRIEF: The client recognized a consumer gap for new premium-quality savoury snacks and wished to capitalize upon this; to create a total concept and brand name for the range; to provide a distinctive presentation, emotive of the speciality snacks within. To create the premium snack brand in this competitive market.

DESIGN RATIONALE: Speciality snacks based on expert baking techniques, hence the choice of name for the range: Baker's Street. Each product shows a different shop front with an individual character. The packs are free-standing, creating a row of ethnic shops. It has a distinctive, recognizable identity, relevant to the product inside.

DKNY Tee Bag

CLIENT: DKNY, New York, USA

DESCRIPTION OF PRODUCT: 11½" × 14" kraft paper

DESIGNER: Arnell Bickford Associates Marketing, New York, USA

DATE OF COMPLETION: December 1991

TARGET MARKET: DKNY customers

PLACE OF SALE: DKNY boutiques in department stores – Bloomingdales and Saks

CLIENT'S BRIEF: To find a novel approach to the packaging and marketing of tee shirts year-round, but particularly during the holiday season.

DESIGN RATIONALE: The DKNY Tee Bag is a practical, visual pun. The tee is enclosed in a porous liner that is stapled closed and connected by a string to a perforated label in the outer packaging. The DKNY Tee Bag eliminates giftwrapping, is humorous and serves as a billboard for the DKNY logo.

Duvet Box

CLIENT: Dorma, Manchester, UK

DESCRIPTION OF PRODUCT: Goose or duck down duvet

DESIGNER: Colin Sands, Lynn Trickett & Brian Webb,
Trickett & Webb, London, UK

TARGET MARKET: Mass markets, predominantly women

PLACE OF SALE: Department stores

CLIENT'S BRIEF: To design an up-market duvet box to
contain either a gooose or duck down duvet.

DESIGN RATIONALE: A *trompe l'oeil* basket was
designed and a goose down or duck down label was
applied as appropriate.

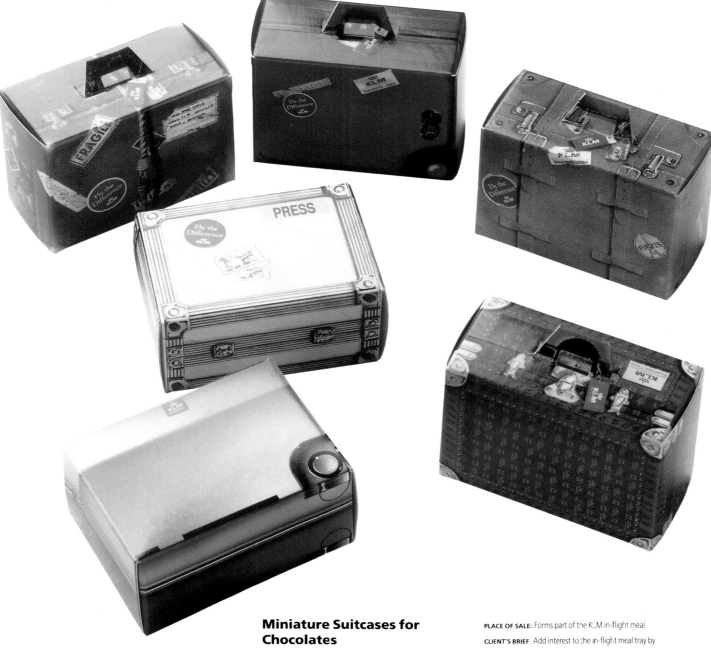

Miniature Suitcases for Chocolates

CLIENT: KLM Royal Dutch Airlines, Amstelveen, The Netherlands

DESCRIPTION OF PRODUCT: Range of individual "suitcases" for just one chocolate

DESIGNER: Packaging Innovation Ltd, London, UK

DATE OF COMPLETION/PRODUCT LAUNCH: November 1991

TARGET MARKET: Business class/first class air travellers

PLACE OF SALE: Forms part of the KLM in-flight meal

CLIENT'S BRIEF: Add interest to the in-flight meal tray by repackaging the chocolate.

DESIGN RATIONALE: The suitcase theme was based on the premise that other people's suitcases arouse curiosity – telling a miniature story about its owner. They come in nine different eye-catching designs ranging from a battered old suitcase typically used by a hiker to a sophisticated Louis Vuitton style – with the familiar LV logo cheekily changed to that of Packaging Innovation.

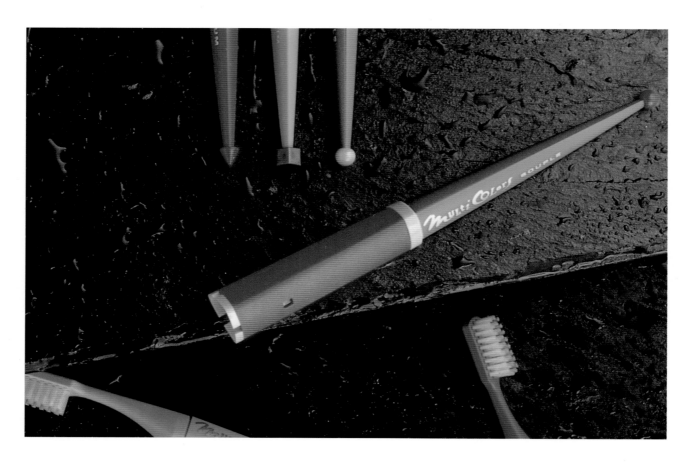

Les Multicolors

CLIENT: Laboratoires Goupil, Rungis, France

DESCRIPTION OF PRODUCT: Range of 12 toothbrushes in six colours and three different caps

DESIGNER: Raison Pure, Paris, France

DATE OF COMPLETION/PRODUCT LAUNCH: February 1992

TARGET MARKET: All the family – aged 7 to 77

PLACE OF SALE: Chemist's shops

CLIENT'S BRIEF: To create a toothbrush that would literally invite people to brush their teeth, and to make the activity attractive to the whole family.

DESIGN RATIONALE: To create a new kind of cap that made loading the toothbrush with paste easier, and to make the brush itself more aesthetically attractive.

Fluocaril Toothpaste

CLIENT: Goupil-Fluocaril, Rungis, France

DESCRIPTION OF PRODUCT: Plastic: height 20cm; plastic stand: height 5cm, width 5.5cm

DESIGNER: Philippe Starck, Paris, France

ILLUSTRATOR/PHOTOGRAPHER: Herve Ternisien

DATE OF COMPLETION/PRODUCT LAUNCH: September 1990

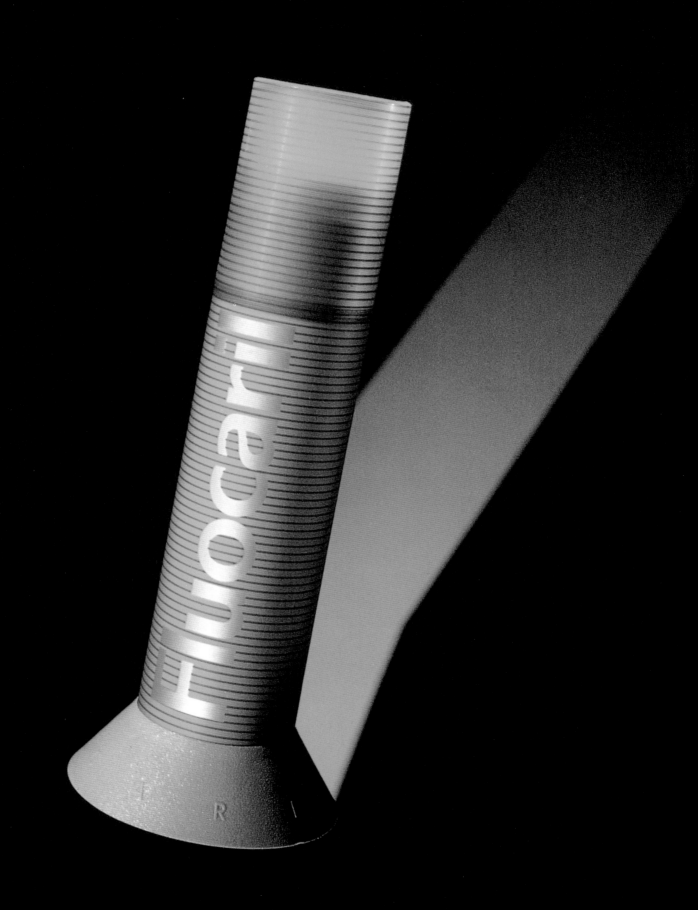

Spätburgunder Rosé Brut

CLIENT: Weingut Georg Messer GmbH & Co,
Weisenheim am Berg, Germany

DESCRIPTION OF PRODUCT: Rosé sparkling wine in dark
green designer bottle, packed in metal gift box

DESIGNER: Georg Messer, Klaus Dieter Freund, Tristan
Pranjko, Weisenheim am Berg, Germany

DATE OF COMPLETION/PRODUCT LAUNCH: 1989

TARGET MARKET: Discerning wine drinkers

PLACE OF SALE: Delicatessen shops, restaurants,
designer shops and high-quality stores

CLIENT'S BRIEF: Germany has a number of high-quality
manufacturers of sparkling wine. Our wine estate
wanted the product to take its place as a top-quality
product, helped by the designer packaging and bottles.

DESIGN RATIONALE: Bottles and packaging are not only
a means of transport and protection but also a cultural
expression of the time as well as being an important part
in social life. Our "Méthode Messer" contributes to
make wine a visual attraction and wine drinking a social
event.

1988 Spätburgunder Rosé Spätlese trocken

CLIENT: Weingut Georg Messer GmbH & Co, Weisenheim am Berg, Germany

DESCRIPTION OF PRODUCT: Rosé wine in a Bordeaux bottle

DESIGNER: Georg Messer, Klaus Dieter Freund, Tristan Pranjko, Weisenheim am Berg, Germany

DATE OF PRODUCT LAUNCH: 1989

TARGET MARKET: Discerning clients

PLACE OF SALE: Delicatessen shops, restaurants, designer shops, high-quality stores worldwide

CLIENT'S BRIEF: The location of our vineyards with their most diverse soils allow us to grow a variety of classical grapes at the highest possible quality standard.

DESIGN RATIONALE: Bottles and packaging are not only a means of transport and protection but also a cultural expression of the time as well as being an important part in social life. Our "Methode Messer" contributes to make wine a visual attraction and wine drinking a social event.

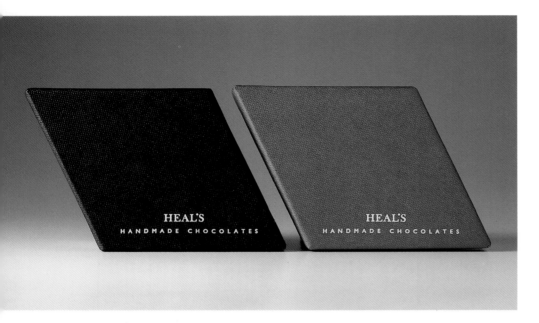

Heal's Handmade Chocolates

CLIENT: Heal's, London, UK

DESCRIPTION OF PRODUCT: Handmade chocolates

DESIGNER: Jimmy Yang, Lewis Moberly, London, UK

DATE OF COMPLETION/PRODUCT LAUNCH: November 1991

TARGET MARKET: Quality shoppers

PLACE OF SALE: Heal's (quality furnishing, household accessories and specialist food store), London, UK

CLIENT'S BRIEF: To design packaging that reflected the product quality and the store's reputation for integrity, economy in design and attention to detail.

DESIGN RATIONALE: The box is diamond-shaped with a ribbon detail to open the lid. It creates the opportunity for striking in-store displays. The shape, subtle use of colour, and "minimalist" approach to graphics reflect the store's discerning style.

A Chauffeur's Reflections

CLIENT: Boots, Nottingham, England

DESCRIPTION OF PRODUCT: Carcare kit – sponge/ chamois, shampoo, etc

DESIGNER: Trickett & Webb Ltd, London, UK

ILLUSTRATOR: Paul Leith

DATE OF COMPLETION: Autumn 1985

TARGET MARKET: Men of all shapes, sizes, ages and types – but often bought by women and children

PLACE OF SALE: Boots chain of stores

CLIENT'S BRIEF: To create a range of packaging for a group of small gift products (with nothing in common) to be given to men for Christmas.

DESIGN RATIONALE: We created a library of "books" to contain each gift item. Each book was designed within a particular genre, linked to the character of the product. Cover illustrations were commissioned from appropriate illustrators – as for 'real' book jackets.

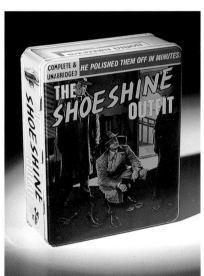

The Shoeshine Outfit

CLIENT: Boots, Nottingham, England

DESCRIPTION OF PRODUCT: Shoecare kit – brushes, dusters, polish, etc

DESIGNER: Trickett & Webb Ltd, London, UK

ILLUSTRATOR: Mark Thomas

DATE OF COMPLETION: Autumn 1985

TARGET MARKET: Men of all shapes, sizes, ages and types – but often bought by women and children

PLACE OF SALE: Boots chain of stores

A Close Shave in Piccadilly

CLIENT: Boots, Nottingham, England

DESCRIPTION OF PRODUCT: Shaving kit – shaving brush, china soap dish, soap

DESIGNER: Trickett & Webb Ltd, London, UK

ILLUSTRATOR: Jeff Cummins

DATE OF COMPLETION: Autumn 1985

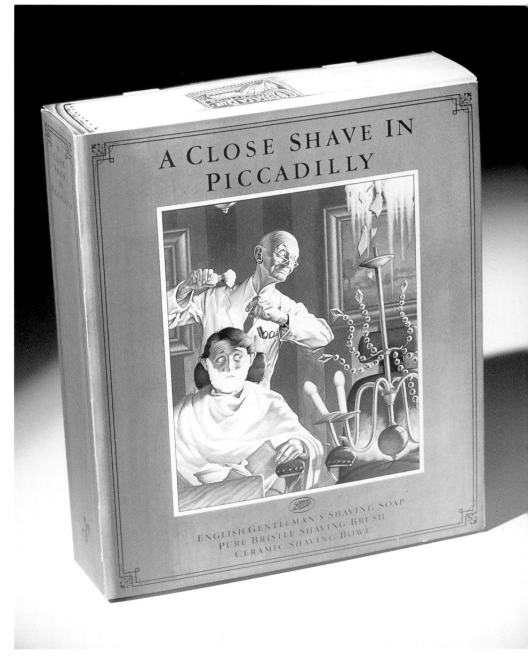

Fine Food Book

CLIENT: The Duchess of Devonshire, Chatsworth, Derbyshire

DESCRIPTION OF PRODUCT: Gift pack for jams, pickles and so on, to look as if part of the famous Chatsworth House

DESIGNER: Stuart Colville, Ian Logan Design Co, London, UK

ILLUSTRATOR: Matthew Cook

DATE OF COMPLETION/PRODUCT LAUNCH: 1991

TARGET MARKET: Promotional gift pack for high-class food shops

PLACE OF SALE: Chatsworth, Harrods and high-quality food shops

CLIENT'S BRIEF: To design a gift box for various items in a range of fine foods. The intention was to attract catalogue buyers.

DESIGN RATIONALE: We considered, as with all the range, to bring Chatsworth close to all the foods in that they would be an extension of the promotion of the house.

Natural Beauty Soap

CLIENT: Ian Logan, London, UK

DESCRIPTION OF PRODUCT: Vegetable soap in decorated tin boxes inside presentation gift box (handmade)

DESIGNER: Ian Logan, Ian Logan Design Company, London, UK

ILLUSTRATOR: Francesca Palazolli

DATE OF COMPLETION/PRODUCT LAUNCH: 1990

TARGET MARKET: Upper end of fine toiletries market

PLACE OF SALE: Toiletries department in high-class department stores

CLIENT'S BRIEF: To provide a range of fine vegetable toiletry products, with only natural fragrances.

DESIGN RATIONALE: The packaging had to be good enough and sufficiently different for the customer to want to keep it.

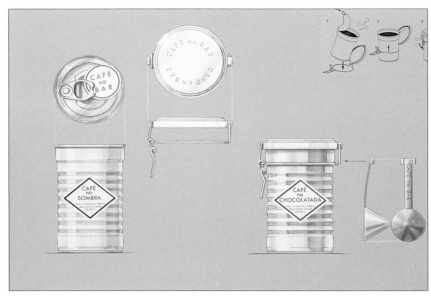

Café no Bar

CLIENT: Mitsubishi Corporation, Tokyo, Japan

DESCRIPTION OF PRODUCT: Aluminium capsule

DESIGNER: GK Graphics Incorporated, Tokyo, Japan

DATE OF COMPLETION/PRODUCT LAUNCH: December 1988

TARGET MARKET: National brand, department store

PLACE OF SALE: Japan

DESIGN RATIONALE: To introduce the product to the gourmet gift market. The design employs an aluminium capsule, for the first time for its kind, designed to express a futuristic image of fancy and precious content and also an effective seal. In order to make the user aware that it is precious, the capacity is smaller than regular coffee packages.

Café Citio (Series)

CLIENT: Morinaga Milk Industry Co Ltd, Tokyo, Japan

DESCRIPTION OF PRODUCT: Coffee in packs. The materials are aluminium, with a paper label. Net weight is 200g

DESIGNER: Taku Satoh, Tokyo, Japan

DATE OF PRODUCT LAUNCH: December 1988

TARGET MARKET: Young people who like living in a city

PLACE OF SALE: Throughout Japan

CLIENT'S BRIEF: Three regular coffees are blended in three ways such as a "Blend for Hospitality", "Blend for Relaxation" and "Normal Blend". They are also suitable as gifts.

DESIGN RATIONALE: To deliver the original taste of coffee, the quality feeling of the metal (aluminium) pack was used in the can's surface.

Tactile

All of our senses are involved when we are looking at, and handling, packaging — but perhaps the one most often overlooked is our sense of touch. Texture not only helps to evoke richness and dimension when we touch a product, but it also enhances some of the qualities of the contents. The texture of orange peel on orange juice bottles, the smoothness of silk on shampoo bottles, or the roughness of drawing paper for artist's materials are all examples of this quality.

But texture also affects the way that light plays across a surface, so it can have a visual impact as well. Embossed patterns on glassware affect the way that light passes through the contents, and gives an added sparkle and a feeling of quality.

Conversely, if texture helps to make the product more practical — if it is easier to grip, or if the heavy container does not slip from our hands as we pour oil into our car engines — we are more likely to remember the product and buy it regularly.

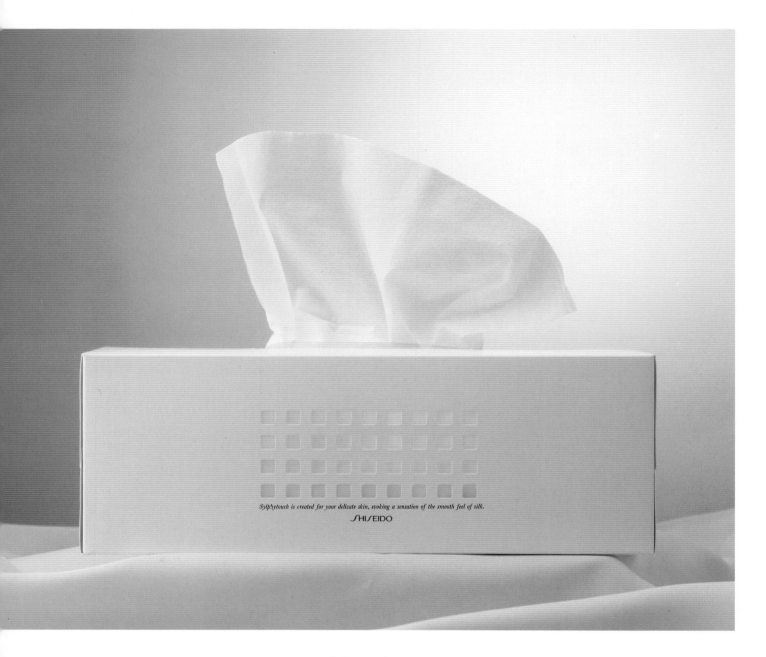

Sylphtouch is created for your delicate skin, evoking a sensation of the smooth feel of silk.

SHISEIDO

Sylphtouch tissues

CLIENT: Shiseido Co Ltd, Tokyo, Japan

DESCRIPTION OF PRODUCT: Paper cosmetic utensil

DESIGNER: Tetsuo, Togasawa, Tokyo, Japan

DATE OF COMPLETION/PRODUCT LAUNCH: August, 1990

TARGET MARKET: All

PLACE OF SALE: Shiseido chain stores

DESIGN RATIONALE: As distinct from other tissues on market, these are for cosmetic purposes; the tissues are for wiping-off make-up. They are extremely soft to the skin. Nowadays tissues are a basic necessity of life. The package box was designed to be moderate but also attractive, and to harmonize with interiors.

Berol Pencils

CLIENT: Berol Ltd, London, UK

DESCRIPTION OF PRODUCT: Range of packaging for pencils and crayons

DESIGNER: Newell and Sorrell, London, UK

DATE OF COMPLETION/PRODUCT LAUNCH: 1990

TARGET MARKET: Craft and gift market

PLACE OF SALE: Art and craft stores, stationers, department stores

Melrose's Fresh Roasted Coffee

CLIENT: Granton, Edinburgh, Scotland

DESCRIPTION OF PRODUCT: Design of bags and labels for 16 blends of Fresh Ground Coffee (various sizes) plus point of sale material. Brand identity required

DESIGNER: Graphic Partners, Edinburgh, Scotland

ILLUSTRATOR: Rosamund Fowler

DATE OF COMPLETION/PRODUCT LAUNCH: March 1990

TARGET MARKET: ABC1 25–44 year olds

PLACE OF SALE: Delicatessens

CLIENT'S BRIEF: To re-establish Melrose's Fresh Roasted Coffee and create a brand identity. Pack imagery to be in line with both traditional delicatessens and modern superstores.

DESIGN RATIONALE: The design solution reflects a quality product proposition. The metallic silver base-colour emphasizes the feeling of freshness. To warm up the image, copper, cream and full-colour illustration were used. Embossed and printed coffee beans were employed as a graphic device on the metallic items to suggest the full flavour of the bean bursting through the material. One generic illustration was used to build brand identity.

Brannigan's Beer Nuts

CLIENT: KP Foods, London, UK

DESCRIPTION OF PRODUCT: Nuts roasted in their skins and coated with salt

DESIGNER: Coley Porter Bell, London, UK

ILLUSTRATOR: Brian Saunders

TARGET MARKET: Teenagers to adults, male and female

PLACE OF SALE: Public houses, supermarkets

CLIENT'S BRIEF: Brannigans is a premium snack launched by KP Foods in 1989. KP wanted to develop a brand that could be extended across a range of products while appealing to the increasingly important adult market. Targeting the under 45-year-old housewife buying for herself and her partner, the brand's central proposition – its traditional, home-cooked flavour – is at the heart of its identity.

DESIGN RATIONALE: Packs feature "Mr Brannigan", a 1920's New York delicatessen owner, depicted in Norman Rockwell-style illustration with turn-of-the-century typography. Coley Porter Bell rejected the foil pillow bags used by the majority of snacks in favour of brown paper, flat-bottomed packs sealed across the top. This seemingly simple choice of packaging created a unique distinction between Brannigans and other premium snacks.

Nactalia

CLIENT: Eurial, Nantes, France

DESCRIPTION OF PRODUCT: Plastic milk bottle

DESIGNER: Lonsdale Design, Boulogne, France

DATE OF COMPLETION/PRODUCT LAUNCH: 1991

TARGET MARKET: Milk consumers aware of their health

PLACE OF SALE: Big stores and supermarkets

CLIENT'S BRIEF: To enhance the range of this new brand "Nactalia" with original packaging, while avoiding giving the bottle an overly technological aspect.

Florida Orange Juice

CLIENT: County Dairies Fruit Juices, Kidlington, Oxford, UK

DESCRIPTION OF PRODUCT: 500ml-bottle containing 100% freshly squeezed Florida orange juice

DESIGNER: Jarvis White, Tetbury, Glos.

DATE OF PRODUCT LAUNCH: March 1992

TARGET MARKET: Primarily adults; consumers who appreciate the unsurpassed flavour quality of freshly squeezed juice in general, and who will enjoy the naturally sweeter and smoother character of this juice derived solely from Florida oranges.

PLACE OF SALE: The chiller cabinet in major supermarket multiples

CLIENT'S BRIEF: To provide artwork and illustration for the production of a 500ml label, to emphasize the unusual Florida origins of this freshly squeezed orange juice, and to add interest and variety in the chiller cabinet to promote this seasonally available juice.

DESIGN RATIONALE: To originate a label format possessing a strong Floridan character, giving good differentiation and stand-out on shelf; reiterating the unique selling points of "first choice" freshly squeezed Florida orange juice, using typical Florida imagery – everglades, sun, sea, warmth, etc.

Fortant de France

CLIENT: Grange Skalli, Sète, France

DESCRIPTION OF PRODUCT: 75cl glass bottle, Bordeaux-style, with a bunch of grapes in relief

DESIGNER: Alain Carré Design Étude, Paris, France

DATE OF COMPLETION/PRODUCT LAUNCH: 1989

TARGET MARKET: Hotels and restaurants and as collector's item

CLIENT'S BRIEF: To create an international design with a strong, memorable image

DESIGN RATIONALE: The use of the bunch of grapes in relief on the bottle gives the product special appeal. The image had to be strong enough for the bottles to be bought 'blind'.

Giardini

CLIENT: HP Bulmer Limited, Hereford, UK

DESCRIPTION OF PRODUCT: A soft drink comprising herbs and fruit juice

DESIGNER: Fisher Ling & Bennion Limited, Cheltenham, Glos, UK

ILLUSTRATOR/PHOTOGRAPHER: Javier Sanchez

DATE OF COMPLETION/PRODUCT LAUNCH: 1991

TARGET MARKET: Adults, but probably mainly females

PLACE OF SALE: Supermarkets, off-licences, health food shops and grocery stores

CLIENT'S BRIEF: To develop a brand identity and packaging for a new soft drink consisting of herbs and fruit juice. The product is aimed at adults, mainly women, and is positioned as an alternative to alcohol and mineral water

DESIGN RATIONALE: Fisher Ling & Bennion was asked to produce the total concept for a new drink. This involved the development of the name, brand identity and bottle design. The name "Giardini", which is Italian for garden, and the brand identity position the product as an aspirational, healthy and enjoyable drink. The use of blue glass reflects purity and water, whilst the embossed imagery symbolizes the herbal and fruit ingredients.

Savonne Imported Wines

CLIENT: Glendinning Associates, for Savin S.A., Westport, CT, USA

DESCRIPTION OF PRODUCT: A bottle that remains within the standard wine bottle contour but incorporates a unique faceted helix that starts at the top and swirls around the entire bottle

DESIGNER: Gerstman+Meyers Inc, New York, USA

DATE OF PRODUCT LAUNCH: October 1988

TARGET MARKET: Wine consumers

PLACE OF SALE: Liquor stores in selected markets throughout the United States

CLIENT'S BRIEF: This leading European winemaker wanted to introduce a line of still wine products to the US market that would compete on a national basis with high-volume wines such as Canei, Cella, Blue Nun and Bolla. Introducing new products in this market segment is risky, with a high failure ratio. Distinctive bottles and labels were needed in order for this new product introduction to be successful.

DESIGN RATIONALE: Gerstman+Meyers developed a wine bottle silhouette with proprietary moulded swirls for elegance and uniqueness. The labels for the Savonne brand utilize an elegant diamond shape, which provides shelf impact and strong family identity. The wine varieties are differentiated by label background colours and the overall imagery meets the objective of high quality and affordability.

Evian

CLIENT: Société-des-Eaux Minérales d'Evian, France

DESCRIPTION OF PRODUCT: A special edition Evian bottle; glass is shaped from a single block and embellished with a silkscreen design

DESIGNER: Style Marque – Christiana Sofianopou-Lou, Jean Pierre, Carolina Neon, Paris, France

DATE OF COMPLETION/PRODUCT LAUNCH: November 1991

PLACE OF SALE: Some selected supermarkets (such as Galeries Lafayette "Gourmet" and Monoprix)

CLIENT'S BRIEF: To celebrate the Winter Games of which they were a sponsor, Evian asked the designers to create a special edition Evian bottle.

DESIGN RATIONALE: To capture the purity of the Alps, Evian's home, very clear glass was used to mirror the purity of the water. The design had to emphasize the product's qualities and make an impact at both the time of purchase and the time of consumption.

Territorial House Salsas

CLIENT: Pace Foods, San Antonio, TX, USA

DESCRIPTION OF PRODUCT: Pot-shaped glass jars in various sizes

DESIGNER: Gerstman+Meyers Inc, New York, USA

DATE OF COMPLETION/PRODUCT LAUNCH: August 1990

TARGET MARKET: Salsas consumers

PLACE OF SALE: Grocery stores in selected markets throughout the United States

CLIENT'S BRIEF: Territorial House, originally the name of a well-known Sante Fe restaurant, was heralded for its unique salsas. In order to merchandize the products at retail outlets, an effective brand image was needed to project their south-west authenticity.

DESIGN RATIONALE: Gerstman+Meyers developed brand imagery through label graphics and a jar which is functional for spooning and unique in its south-west shape and detailing. The label motif complements the jars, using colours, patterns, and an illustration that reflects the heritage of the products. Brand recognition is immediate and the flavours are differentiated through colour-coded labels and caps.

Floral Bath Range

CLIENT: J Sainsbury PLC, London, UK

DESCRIPTION OF PRODUCT: Bathroom toiletries –
shower cream, soap, bath oil and talc (6 fragrances)

DESIGNER: Bottles, Planet (Jan Webb); Graphics,
Worthington & Co (Andrew Swain), London, UK

DATE OF COMPLETION/PRODUCT LAUNCH: January 1992

TARGET MARKET: Women in the 25–50 age group

PLACE OF SALE: Sainsbury's multiple stores

CLIENT'S BRIEF: To complement the unique Egyptian
design of the bottle while retaining the floral reference
to the product range.

DESIGN RATIONALE: Simple, uncluttered graphics with
hieroglyphic look with symbolistic floral ornamentation.

Bokma Jonge Korenwijn
(Young Cornwine)

CLIENT: Bols Benelux BV, The Netherlands

DESCRIPTION OF PRODUCT: A 1-litre square, sand-blasted, glass bottle. The plastic seal has been carefully detailed to give the appearance of an original wax seal

DESIGNER: Eugene Bay, Marcel Gort, Visser Bay Anders Toscani, Amsterdam, The Netherlands

DATE OF COMPLETION/PRODUCT LAUNCH: September 1987

TARGET MARKET: Professional males from 35 to 50

PLACE OF SALE: Off-licences and supermarkets; cafes and bars

CLIENT'S BRIEF: To create a premium-quality Dutch genever. This product must act as a catalyst for other products that fall under the brand name "Bokma". It is a first step in repositioning the total product range up-market.

DESIGN RATIONALE: This top-grade Dutch genever has been designed to reflect quality through simplicity. The 1-litre square bottle, synonymous with this brand, has been sand-blasted, reflecting the way this drink should be served: ice-cold.

Purdey's

CLIENT: Callitheke, Harlow, Essex, UK

DESCRIPTION OF PRODUCT: Sparkling herbal multivitamin drink (25 cl; glass; shrinkwrap)

DESIGNER: Callitheke, Harlow, Essex, UK

DATE OF COMPLETION/PRODUCT LAUNCH: 1989

TARGET MARKET: Men and women aged 15 to 30, ABC1, C2; style leaders

PLACE OF SALE: National chemist, grocery, health specialist distribution, nightclubs, bars

DESIGN RATIONALE: The product had to look space-age, and appear stylish, unique and distinctive.

Old Jamaican

CLIENT: Government of Jamaica, Kingston, Jamaica

DESCRIPTION OF PRODUCT: Two container types – straw for dry foods and ceramic for liquids – for spices, coffee, preserves and sauces

DESIGNER: Robert P. Gersin Associates, New York, USA

ILLUSTRATOR: Angela Staples

TARGET MARKET: Tourists and exporters

PLACE OF SALE: Tourist gift shops in Jamaica and Bloomingdale's Gourmet Foods Department

CLIENT'S BRIEF: To create a package that would convey a uniquely Jamaican character. The containers had to meet FDA approval for export to the USA, and were to be made as part of a job/skills programme.

DESIGN RATIONALE: To create a mark for the brand "Old Jamaican" that could be applied to future products.

Ténéré

CLIENT: Paco Rabanne Parfums SA, Neuilly sur-Seine, France

DESCRIPTION OF PRODUCT: Ténéré eau de toilette, 8 × 12 × 2.5cm, crystal and plastic for men

DESIGNER: Andre Ricard, Barcelona, Spain

DATE OF COMPLETION/PRODUCT LAUNCH: 1989

TARGET MARKET: Males

PLACE OF SALE: Perfume stores

CLIENT'S BRIEF: A new eau de toilette to complete Paco Rabanne's line, addressed to a younger, sporting clientele.

DESIGN RATIONALE: Bottle and cap form a compact shape and are easily gripped.

BP Oil

CLIENT: BP Oil, London, UK

DESCRIPTION OF PRODUCT: BP Oil packaging

DESIGNER: Garrick Hamm (Art Director: Glenn Tutssel), Michael Peters, London, UK

DATE OF COMPLETION/PRODUCT LAUNCH: June 1991

TARGET MARKET: 25–35-year-old male drivers

PLACE OF SALE: Service stations/garages

CLIENT'S BRIEF: To create a distinctive package design whose style reflects that of the user.

DESIGN RATIONALE: The ergonomic shape helps handling and pourability. The snap-off top conceals the pouring spout which has anti-glug and non-drip details. The unique styling and grips create a perfect functional pack.

Nature et Découverte

CLIENT: François Leoarchand, Nature et Découverte, Paris, France

DESCRIPTION OF PRODUCT: Boxes and craft bag in paper

DESIGNER: Agora, Paris, France

DATE OF PRODUCT LAUNCH: 1991

TARGET MARKET: The general public

PLACE OF SALE: Nature et Découverte shops

CLIENT'S BRIEF: To create a design that complemented the colours and textures of nature.

DESIGN RATIONALE: To get consumers to think more carefully about nature and its implications for us all.

Grapefruit Range

CLIENT: Czech & Speake Ltd, London, UK

DESCRIPTION OF PRODUCT: Unisex fragrance in boxes of white (revealed), corrugated card with splashes of red, yellow and orange squares, complemented by white-on-red labels

DESIGNER: Czech & Speake Ltd, London, UK

DATE OF COMPLETION/PRODUCT LAUNCH: October 1991

TARGET MARKET: Aimed at the 20–40 age group. A vibrant, fresh fragrance for both men and women. It is international in feel

PLACE OF SALE: Retail shop and wholesale market in UK, Europe, USA and Japan

CLIENT'S BRIEF: The product was developed mainly for the younger market as a unisex fragrance that would be of particular appeal during the warmer months. The fragrance is much favoured by the sportsmen and women, who used the "Splash" as a refreshing light fragrance after sports. However, the fragrance appeals just as much to the mature international man, who wants a light, citrus-toned daily cologne splash. It is a refreshing, bright, lemony fragrance with a zest that is reflected in the packaging.

DESIGN RATIONALE: The packaging is unique, and has rarely been seen anywhere else in this format. The outer carton wall was reversed out so that the white corrugated board was displayed in full. This idea is so original that the design has been registered as a new design concept. In order to emphasize the youthful image of the fragrance, Czech & Speake enlarged the packaging design to include red, yellow and orange splashes of colour on the outer casing. This fragrance range is now the second-best seller, despite the fact that resources and finance for the project and overall design development were very limited.

Index of Projects

Directory of Practising Designers

This directory lists the addresses of designers in current practice. While every effort has been made to ensure that this list was correct at the time of going to press, subsequent changes in address or status are beyond the publishers' remit.

Bob Adamski
118 Boulevard Richard Lenoir
Paris 75011
France
PROJECT: Doré and Doré Socks 86

Addison Design Consultants
60 Britton Street
London EC1M 5NA
England
PROJECT: Purina pet accessories 35

Agora
36 rue Fontaine
Paris 75009
France
PROJECT: Nature et Decouverte 220

Albion Botanical
Botanica Park
St Neot's Road
Hardwick
Cambridge CB3 7QL
England
PROJECTS: Seashore 55; Wild Lily 56; Potpourri 57

Ardi
Méré Montfort l'Amaury
France
PROJECT: Packaging 166

Arnell Bickford Associates
100 Grand Street
New York
NY 10013
USA
PROJECT: DKNY Tee Bag 185

Ateliers Dinand
12 rue Carnot
Levallois-Perret 92300
France
PROJECTS: Antarctic 103; Obsession 105; 8e jour 112; Volupté d'Oscar de la Renta 113; Escape by Calvin Klein 124; Arrogantissima 125; El Chanro 126; Liz Claiborne 172; Krazy de Krizia 173; Teatro alla Scala 181

Ateliers Réunis Bagnolet
214 rue Étienne Marcel
Bagnolet 93170
France

Graham Barker
Manor Farm
Adstone
Towcester
Northants NN12 8DT
England
PROJECT: Boxed wine or port 161

Big Active Ltd
Warehouse D4/Riverside
Metropolitan Wharf
Wapping Wall
London E1 9SS
England
PROJECT: Best Direction jeans 88

Blackburn's Ltd
16 Carlisle Street
London W1V 5RE
England
PROJECTS: Cutty Sark whisky 76; Old Parr Elizabethan whisky 79; Baker Street Snacks 184

Bull Rodger Ltd
9 Paddington Street
London W1M 3LA
PROJECT: Beastro 146

Alain Carré Design Étude
11 rue Paul Lelong
Paris 75002
France
PROJECTS: Lacoste pour Homme 41; Fortant de France 208

Chermayeff & Geismar Inc
15 East 26 Street
New York, NY 10010
USA
PROJECTS: Liz Claiborne for Men 00; Realities 177

Le Clan Design
61 rue Servan
75011 Paris
France
PROJECT: Arthur & Lola 178

Cofci SA
Paris
France
PROJECT: Laguna 182

Coley Porter Bell
4 Flitcroft Street
London WC2 8DS
PROJECTS: Ostlers Biscuits 37; J. Additions 42; Lutz 68; Aspects 69; Washing Powder Liquid 132; Brannigan's Beer Nuts 204

Consumer Promotions Inc
633 S. Fulton Avenue
Mount Vernon
New York, NY 10550
USA
PROJECTS: Cartier Parfum 183

Desgrippes Gato Gobe Group
18 bis Avenue de la Motte-Picquet
Paris, 75007
France
PROJECTS: Molto Missoni 24; Boucheron 25; Vichy pastilles 72; Tahiti shower gel 155; Le Coutances cheese; Vie Privée 182

Dieter Bakic Design
Via GC Procaccini 6
21100 Varese
Italy
PROJECTS: Noevir 95

Disseny i Communicacio Ideograma SA
Balmes 52, 2n1a
Barcelona 08007
Spain
PROJECT: Nou Telèfon, Nou Fax 168

Dragon Rouge/Wellcom
249 rue St Jacques
75005 Paris
France
PROJECTS: Acaciane 102; Novemail Plus 135; Star 176

Ekonos
40 rue d'église
Paris XVe
France
PROJECT: S de Savanne 106

Estudio Ricard
Capitan Aranas 3, bajos
08034 Barcelona
Spain

Fisher Ling & Bennion Ltd
Glenmore Lodge
Wellington Square
Cheltenham
Glos. GL50 4NY
England
PROJECTS: Giardini 209; Letters, Numbers, Misfits 150

Robert P. Gersin Associates
11 East 22nd Street
New York, NY 10010
USA
PROJECT: Old Jamaican 217

Gerstman & Meyers Inc
111 West 57th Street
New York, NY 10019
USA
PROJECTS: Real deodorant 154; Savonne Imported Wine 210; Territorial House Salsas 212

GK Graphics Inc
Yamatane Bldg 8F
1.11.22 Minami-Ikebukuro
Toshinaku
Tokyo
Japan
PROJECTS: Café Premio 116; Café No Bar 198

Graphic Partners
Gladstone Court
179 Canongate
Edinburgh EH8 88N
Scotland
PROJECTS: Arran provisions 15; Glencadarn whisky 77; Proposed perfume range 80; Melrose's Fresh Roasted Coffee 205

Grosvenor of London plc
49 Marylebone High Street
London W1M 3AD
England
PROJECT: Thomas the Tank Engine 60

Henkel KGaA
D-4000
Düsseldorf
Germany
PROJECT: Pritt Bastelkleber 123

Peter Hobbs Design Associates
Studio 4
3 Grove Road
Richmond
Surrey TW10 6SP
England
PROJECT: Shoecare kit 63

The Jenkins Group
London
England
PROJECT: Speciality Teas 38

Jones & Co Design Ltd
Greenland Studio
9 Greenland Street
London NW1 0ND
England
PROJECT: Lunchbox 170

Kontrapunkt
11 Garrick Street
London WC2E 9AR
England
PROJECT: Carluccios 31

Kosé Corporation
3.6.2 Nihonbashi
Chuo-Ky
Tokyo
Japan
PROJECT: Self-conscious 102

Thierry Lecoule Design
42 rue Eugène Carrière
Paris 75018
France
PROJECTS: Beauté Capillaire 73; Night & Day: Griesser 127; Vie Vessace 180

Light & Coley Design Consultants
20 Fulham Broadway
London SW6 1AH
England
PROJECT: Aspects 69

Graham Lincoln
2 Spencer Parade
Northampton NN1 3AA
England
PROJECT: Asda oils 17

Ian Logan Design
42 Charterhouse Square
London EC1M 6EU
England
PROJECTS: Fine Food Book 196; Natural Beauty Soap 197

The London Design Partnership
The Work
Torriano Mews
Torriano Avenue
London
England
PROJECT: Bubble Bath 149

Lonsdale Design
78 Bd de la République
92514 Boulogne Billancourt
France
PROJECTS: Fruité 138; Nactalia 206

MBD Groupe Design
11 rue Victor Hugo
Bagnolet 93177
France
PROJECT: Chocolates Valrhona 74

Miller et Bertaux
17 rue Ferdinand Duval
Paris 75004
France
PROJECT: Gift range 50–54

Millford van den Berg
PO Box 56
2240 Wassenaar
Netherlands
PROJECT: Matisse Yoghurt 110

Minale, Tattersfield & Partners Ltd
The Courtyard
37 Sheen Road
Richmond, Surrey
England
PROJECTS: Valderma Skincare Range 36; Giorgio Armani Swimwear 87; BP2000 Lubricat Range 142

Lewis Mobberley Ltd
33 Gresse Street
London W1P 1PN
England
PROJECTS: Les Huiles Essentielles 22; Linden Lady chocolates 75; Cap Soleil 107; Soltan 128; Oban 160; Heal's handmade chocolates 194

Morrison Dalley Design Partnership
3 Fullham Park Road
London SW6 4LH
England
PROJECT: Essentials 97

Newell & Sorrell
27 St Mary's Road
London NW10 4AS
England
PROJECTS: Boots Haircare range 30; Berol Pencils 203

Lloyd Northover
8 Smart Place
London WC2B 5LW
England
PROJECT: Regime 23

Nucleus Design Ltd
John Loftus House
Summer Road
Thames Ditton
Surrey KT7 0RD
England
PROJECT: Henara 106

Packaging Innovation Ltd
1–5 Colville Mews
Lonsdale Road
London W11 2AR
England
PROJECTS: Les Sensations 134; Jetmax 141; Miniature suitcases for chocolates 187

Pentagram Design Ltd
11 Needham Road
London W11 2RP
England
PROJECT: Trendy men's toiletries 20

Michael Peters
49 Princes Place
London W11 4QA
England
PROJECT: BP Oil 219

Peterson & Blyth Associates
216 East 54th Street
New York, NY 10017
USA
PROJECT: Teenee Beanies 151

Priestman Association
8 World's End Place
London SW10 0HE
England
PROJECT: Pressé folder 152

Primo Angeli Inc
590 Folsom Street
San Francisco
California 94105
USA
PROJECT: Hardenne & Huyse chocolates 39

Printed Matter Ltd
17 Queen Street
Mayfair, London W1
England
PROJECT: Stationery range 59

Raison Pure
38 rue Lantiez
Paris 75017
France
PROJECT: Les Multicolors 188

André Ricard
Barcelona
Spain
PROJECTS: IADA motor oil 140; Ténéré 218

Maurizio di Robilant
36 via Lamarmora
Milano 20122
Italy
PROJECT: Colombia coffee 83

Sams Design
103 Friern Barnet Road
London N11 3EU
England
PROJECT: Puma pill-pots 136

Stadium Design BV
Postbus 408
2180 AK Hillegom
The Netherlands
PROJECT: Andrelon Shampoo 96

Philippe Starck
3 rue de la Roquette
Paris 75014
France
PROJECT: Glacier water bottle 139; Fluocaril 189

Studio Halm
Castroper Str 34
D4690 Herne
The Netherlands
PROJECT: UHU 122; Pritt Bastelkleber 123

Style Marque
10 rue des Moulins
Paris 75001
France
PROJECT: Evian 211

Taku Satoh Design Office Inc
Kobu Tsukiji Bldg 5F
3.10.9 Tsukiji Chuo-ku
Tokyo, Japan 104
PROJECTS: Solea Colotion 98; Max Factor 99; Fec series 100; Maybelline 114; House Days 122; Nikkoh Super Tee Bag 147; Kiyokawa 162; Nikka Whisky 163; Pure Malt 163; Café Citio 199

Tatham Pearce Ltd
9 Hatton Street
London NW8 8PL
England
PROJECT: Account Opening Pack 153

Trickett & Webb
The Factory
84 Marchmont Street
London WC1N 1HE
England
PROJECTS: Duvet box 186; Shaving, shoecare, carcare kits 195

Barrie Tucker Design Pty Ltd
245 Fullerton Road
Eastwood
South Australia 5063
Australia
PROJECTS: Seppelts 100-year-old Para liqueur 70; Angoves Winemakers Limited Edition 70; Morris of Rutherglen 158; Yalumba 159; James Russell Cooler 164; Island Lagers 164; Farmer's Union Cheese and Port 165

UHU Vertriebs GmbH
D-7580 Bühl/Bader
The Netherlands
PROJECTS: UHU Flinke Flasche 123

Via Design
10–12 Carlisle Street
London W1V 5RF
England
PROJECT: Sainsbury's Dishwasher products range 131

Visser Bay Anders Toscani BV
Assumburg 152
Amsterdam
The Netherlands
PROJECTS: Red Band Venco Series 34; Een moment voor jezelf 169; Bokma Jonge Corenwijn 214

Vitrac Design Strategy
60 Rue d'Avron
75020 Paris
France
PROJECTS: Hydra Puissance 94; Free and Free 120; Vitalité 121; Beauté Douce 126; Clicker 171

Bernard Vuarnesson
1 Bld St Michel
Paris 75005
France
PROJECTS: Galilea 167; Pillars of Time 168

Jarvis White
The Old Mill
Mill Lane
Avening
Tetbury, Glos.
England
PROJECT: Fruit juice 00

Worthington & Co
The Tea Warehouse
10A Lant Street
London SE1 1QR
England
PROJECTS: Nature's Compliments 17; Own label tea for Marks & Spencer 82; Antipasto 111; Floral Bath Range 213